TIARA J. HAWTHORNE

PICK UP YOUR
WEAPONS

AND

FIGHT!

DEDICATION

This book is dedicated to all those Christians who have a passionate pursuit for the presence of the Most High God in their lives; those who have been seeking the face of God and who desire to go higher heights and deeper depths in the love of Jesus Christ. This is for those who dare to seek after "the more" of His Holy Spirit.

TABLE OF CONTENTS

BOOT CAMP..9

NO STRIPES ALLOWED...16

YOUR DIET CHANGES...19

PHYSICAL TRAINING (TRIALS AND TESTS)..................25

KNOW YOUR ENEMY..31

EQUIP YOURSELF WITH THE WHOLE ARMOR..............37
    Having Your Loins Girt About With Truth......................37
    Having on the Breastplate of Righteousness..................40
    Feet Shod with the Preparation of the Gospel of Peace....44
    Above All, Taking the Shield of Faith, Wherewith Ye Shall Be Able to Quench All the Fiery Darts of the Wicked...........45
    Taking the Helmet of Salvation..................................48
    Take the Sword of the Spirit, Which is the Word of God 50
    Praying Always with all Supplication......................... 53
PUTTING ON OUR GARMENT OF PRAISE.......................61

FRIENDLY FIRE...66

USE IT OR LOSE IT..73

KILL IT ON CONTACT! ...RECOVER QUICKLY..................83

THE WARFARE..88

NO FEAR OF THE ENEMY..92

THE POWER OF GOD..103

POWER IN ~~NUMBERS~~ (OBEDIENCE)...........................109

BEHIND ENEMY LINES..116

CAMOUFLAGE..121

PROMOTION TO NEXT RANK.......................................126

HONORING THE FALLEN...130
LOVE WORTH DYING FOR...135
AFTERTHOUGHT: THE CHASE...141
PASTOR'S SUGGESTED SUPPLEMENTS............................142
SPIRITUAL WARFARE STUDY GUIDE...............................145

ACKNOWLEDGEMENTS

I thank God through His son Jesus Christ for choosing me to do such a work in Him. I couldn't have dreamed of going such heights and depths to see the spiritual things and revelations that He was willing to share with me as a servant and friend. I am also grateful to my wonderful Husband and best friend who has long suffered and labored with me as the Lord humbled me for such a purpose.

FOREWORD

There is no other way to say things other than to speak matter of fact and straightforward. There was a day that I visited a local church in my neighborhood. I had gone to church before because I wanted to tag-a-long with a friend. Other times, I had gone to church when they had Vacation Bible School because the bus would stop near my home and ask if I wanted to come. The day came when I had to make a choice to serve Jesus Christ and choose Him as my Lord and Savior.

My friend had approached me after Sunday school and asked if I was going to be baptized with them at the next week's service. I said, "Yes", because I wanted to be with my friend. Then the pastor came to me and asked if I believed on the Son, Jesus Christ, and believed that he died and rose for my sins. We prayed the prayer of faith and went to be baptized with my school friend. Though I was persuaded and loved the Lord Jesus Christ with all of my heart, I had no clue how to live for Christ. I would hear the scripture about putting on the whole armor of God and that we wrestle not against flesh and blood. That message was preached numerous times. However, I didn't understand the application of the word concerning spiritual warfare. How do I please the Lord? How do I fight a good fight? What weapon should I use for this situation? When should I use that weapon? How do I overcome? When does that scripture apply? I asked. I needed to do more than fear the Lord. I needed to know Him to serve him properly and be most effective on the spiritual battlefield.

These are my testimonies as I sought the face of God to answer the questions and to learn how to abide in the vine. Numerous times I have come short of the glory of God. I still do. The spiritual warfare is real. He really did die for our sins and rise so that He could have an eternal relationship with us. However, to whom much is given, much is required. These are the accounts that the Lord Jesus allowed to occur so that I could know Him as a Savior and that His refining fire would purify me so that I would be in the position to experience the victory given through Christ Jesus and see His manifest glory in my life through the process. This is how I learned to fight and overcome. I pray that through my testimony you will pick up your weapons and fight to overcome as well.

INTRODUCTION

It took me a while to recognize in my Christian walk that I was a soldier on the battlefield for Christ. For many years, all I could think about was being in the military. Even in my last couple of years in high school, I wanted to be a soldier. Little did I know that I had already been chosen, predestined before I was yet formed in the womb, to fight on the battlefield for the Lord. For me at one point, the military was an obsession. I know that there is some rivalry between branches of the military, but I'll admit that it was the Air Force for me. Everything about it, I longed for. I wanted the uniform, I wanted the guns, I wanted the walk, I wanted the talk, I wanted the ID card, I wanted the decal. I wanted the coins, the travel, and the rank. Think of the absolute smallest thing regarding the military, and I'll tell you that I wanted to be a part of it. How could I know that all of these thoughts and desires within me were pieces to the puzzle the Lord was putting together in my life? Before I had even enlisted in the military, I was already a soldier at heart.

The Lord's Word is absolutely true and does not return void because He said that as the things are in the flesh, so are they also in the spiritual realm. So, though I had wanted to be apart of the US military, in the Spirit, I was already ordained to be in the Lord's army. The difference was that in the military for Christ I went through officer training school, whereas in the flesh I started off as an airman first class. However, whether in the flesh, or in the Spirit, one thing that is certain is that there is always basic training. This is training whether you are drafted or voluntarily enlisted.

For me, I was drafted into the Lord's army. The basic training took a whole lot longer than six weeks. Though hindsight vision is always 20/20, I believe that when I went into basic training, I was in the worst shape I had ever been in. I thought that there was no way I could make it through. However, with God as my drill sergeant, trainer, and commanding officer, the repetition and daily meditations gave me the conditioning that I needed to build strength and endurance.

And ye shall be hated of all men for my names' sake but he that endureth to the end shall be saved.
Matthew 10:22

You cannot go to war without extensive training and preparation. So, as you read this book, I pray that these seeds be planted on fertile ground and sprout up like mustard seeds within you. I also pray that this gives new revelations and insight to my fellow soldiers on the battlefield for Christ as we also reveal many of the devil's strategies, locations, and weapons of mass destruction.

BOOTCAMP

Boot camp is only the start of your walk with Christ. It is your training for the spiritual assignment you've been appointed to do. No matter which branch of the military you're in, there is always a period of preparation and training. One of the first things you do when you arrive to your duty station is get assigned to a squadron or unit, and you're no longer allowed to wear civilian clothing. You are fitted and provided with a uniform. Keep in mind that everything done in the flesh is also done according to a pattern after the things in the spirit. So, true basic training starts upon accepting Christ as your personal Lord and Savior!

So, you're assigned to a unit (church home) and fitted for a uniform (spiritual armor). See, once you're saved, the old clothing has to go.

Therefore, if any man be in Christ, he is a new creature: old things are passed away: behold all things become new.

2Corinthians 5:17

So, you're a new recruit. You have a church that you regularly attend (if not, now would be the time to find somewhere you feel comfortable attending), and you've been given a uniform and armor to go along with it. Be advised that your armor is specifically for you. No one can use your armor and vice versa. Think back on the story of David and Goliath.

...and Saul armed David with his armour, and he put a helmet of brass upon his head; and he armed him with a coat of mail.
And David girded his sword upon his armor, and assayed to go; for he had not proved it. And David said unto Saul, I cannot go with these; for I have not proved them. And David put them off him.   *I Samuel 17:38-39*

The revelation in those scriptures is that the Lord provides us with custom-made armor that is custom made for us only. So, when wartime comes, your armor is well proven.

Put on the whole armour of God, that ye may be able to stand against the wiles of the devil.

For we wrestle not against flesh and blood, but against principalities, against powers, against the rulers of darkness of this world, against spiritual wickedness in high places.

Wherefore take unto you the armour of God, that ye may be able to withstand in the evil day, and having done all, to stand.

Eph 6:11-13

As you can see, when you get to boot camp, you get a new uniform that you wear every day. No longer do you wear civilian clothing. You have been born again. The old things have been passed away.

On a personal note, one thing I learned while in boot camp with the Air Force is that if you do not follow through to the very end or allow stumbling blocks to hinder you along the way, you must go back to the start. In the Air Force, we often called that process, "being recycled."

Throughout each week you are trained on several things, and if you do not pass, then you would be recycled back to the beginning of that week until you could master those things set on that week's agenda. The same exists concerning our spiritual walk. If we do not pass the spiritual tests and trials brought our way, then we must repeat the cycle before moving to our next spiritual level. Just as it was when you were in grade school, you don't get promoted to the next grade level without passing the courses of that level you're already on.

Many of you may have played video games; well, that's another great example! The level that you begin on will continue to repeat itself over and over until you master those things you must accomplish on the first level, then you move on to the next level.

Something else to consider is that if you happen to completely withdraw from training, regardless of what level you're on, and for whatever reason it may be…guess what? You must start over! Unfortunately, you cannot stop and take a break for a while then decide you'll go back to it without starting from square one. You cannot start from where you left off.

When you decide to accept the Love of Jesus Christ and receive him as your personal Lord and Savior; that is the first day of the rest of your eternal life.

John 3:15-16

That whosoever believeth in him should not perish but have eternal life. For God so loved the world he gave his only begotten son, that whosoever believeth in him should not perish, but have everlasting life.

To be clear, this is a huge decision! Recruiters have told us these things over and over. When you think of natural recruiters, think of the Lord's spiritual workers; His Pastors, Evangelists, Prophets, Teachers, and Apostles; those compelling men and women to come to Christ.

They tell you that your life will be different. They say you can impact the lives of others. They also tell you how much you're needed to help protect and serve. Well, Jesus has many of the same expectations, if not more. To whom much is given much is required (Luke 12:48). Once you make the decision to let Jesus Christ have reign in your life completely, it is then that you can understand what boot camp is about.

Boot camp in its simplest form is compiled of three things. Learning who Jesus Christ is to you as three-in-one: Father, Son, and Holy Spirit; and learning the faithfulness that keeps the relationship going for eternity. You learn how the Lord designed you and for what purpose and call. He shows you who He is and how to fear Him with reverence. The word says the fear of the Lord is the beginning of wisdom. With the establishment of His mission and purpose, the Lord Jesus also gives us the example of His will in Jeremiah chapter one.

From the days of old when Moses was leading the children through the wilderness to the place of their inheritance, and also into the days of Joshua, the Lord gave the children the law and a covenant. He gave them also their portion by tribe. The Levites were the priesthood at the time for the children of God. The Lord sanctified them and set them apart for that service. So, we say that to say the priests were raised up with the priests in their portion of land.

The Lord shares with us some of Jeremiah's history. His father's name is Hilkiah who was of the priesthood. He lived in Anatoth located within the land of Benjamin. Because of this information, we know that Jeremiah has some knowledge of God because he grew up amongst a household of priests of the Lord.

The Lord moves to speak to Jeremiah in the days of Josiah while he had already been in the midst of reigning as king of Judah for thirteen years. Josiah was a young king who took the throne at the tender age of eight years old. The word comes when he is twelve years of age. This is not a coincidence that the Lord raises up a young Prophet to prophesy to a young king of the House of Israel.

Before I formed thee, in the belly, I knew thee; and before thou camest forth out of the womb I sanctified thee, and I ordained thee a Prophet unto the nations.
Then said I, ah, Lord God! Behold, I cannot speak: For I am a child.
But the Lord said unto me, say not, I am a child: for thou shalt go to all that I shall send thee, and whatsoever I command thee thou shalt speak.
Be not afraid of their faces: for I am with thee to deliver thee saith the Lord.

Then the Lord put forth his hand and touched my mouth. And the Lord said unto me, behold, I have put my words in thy mouth.
See, I have this day set thee over the nations and over the kingdoms, to root out, and to pull down, and to destroy, and to throw down, to build, and to plant.

      This sets the atmosphere by sharing the spiritual condition with the king. We learn more details of the king in the book of Chronicles and in later chapters. Nonetheless, the Lord doesn't use a messenger in the form of a priest or family member. The Lord God speaks and introduces Himself to Jeremiah directly. He tells him the reason why he came forth and what his purpose for the Lord was even before he was born. The Lord states that before he was formed, he knew him. Meaning, he came forth from the Spirit of God. The priests are sanctified as well, but the Lord specified that he would be called a Prophet and he would be sent forth to the nations to speak as the mouth of God. Each person represents a nation. When he received his call and purpose he is overwhelmed. There's nothing like knowing what your mission and purpose is in this life. Jeremiah gives the Lord some reasoning; one we are so familiar with from the days of Moses who also claimed that he lacked the ability regarding speech. Jeremiah's reasoning with the Lord was his youth.

      He's just a child, he claims. Isn't that interesting of the humility? He questions his own youthfulness while on the other side of things the King Josiah has been reigning since the age of eight, one of the youngest kings we've most likely read about besides King Jesus. The Lord himself addresses this time. Jeremiah suggests that is youth may be considered his weakness. The Lord God makes it clear to the young prophet to not be concerned as if this is a fleshly call. He is in unity by his Spirit to do his will and his purpose. The Lord is with him to do the work.

      So, the Lord gives an introduction, call, purpose, mission, and with this mission a vision because he, being a prophet, is the mouth of God. Jeremiah receives a touch by the Lord as a formal spiritual cleansing and anointing to do the Lord's will effectively and holily. When the Lord gives his purpose; he gives the vision to see it through to the end. Jesus Christ says that he is the author and finisher of our faith. The finishing spirit comes along with the prophetic to know what the future will be for the Lord's chosen. In verse 10, the first thing the Lord mentions is vision. He says, "see I have this day set over thee over the nations and over the kingdoms, to root out, and to pull down, and to destroy, and to throw down, to build and to plant."

Philippians 2:5-7

Let this mind be in you, which was also in Christ Jesus: Who, being in the form of God, thought it not robbery to be equal with God: But made himself of no reputation, and took upon him the form of a servant, and was made in the likeness of men:

Here is the sonship authority. He set him over the nations and kingdoms being in unity by the Spirit of Truth and equal with God. In verse 8, the Lord stated to Jeremiah to be not afraid. He will be with him to deliver him. So, with this prophetic office the Lord also distributes the Spirit of Deliverance to do the work spoken in verse 10 to accomplish his purpose to root out, pull down, to destroy, and to throw down, to build and to plant. Does this sound familiar?

II Corinthians 10:4

For the weapons of our warfare are not carnal, but mighty through God to the pulling down of strongholds; casting down imaginations, and every high thing that exalteth itself against the knowledge of God, and bringing into captivity every thought to the obedience of Christ.

Sometimes, we can think to root out, pull out, or destroy can be a bad thing, but this is the Lord sharing the process of deliverance with his prophet he is sending to the nations. Before a foundation can be laid, there is a tearing down of the old and that which is contrary. When Jesus delivers by his Spirit, he roots out every demonic force. He pulls things form the root. The Lord God does not do anything halfway. He does a complete work. He desires to destroy anything, any enmity that will interfere with his relationship with his children. He must also pull-down vain imaginations spiritual wickedness in high places and anything else that will interfere with the flow of his Spirit. Then, he is able to build and plant seeds of righteousness. The Ground is fertile.

In the beginning of other chapters, we discussed spiritual armor and some of the differences between natural and spiritual.

II Cor 10:3-6

For though we walk in the flesh, we do not war after the flesh: for the weapons of our warfare are not carnal but mighty through God to the pulling down of strong holds, casting down imaginations, and every high thing that exalteth itself against the knowledge of God, and bringing into captivity every thought to the obedience of Christ.

One thing I noticed when I first arrived, I observed many people from different walks of life. Some people enlisted because their recruiter persuaded them of the benefit. Others, felt like it was the only option life presented them. While some stated they were maintaining family tradition because they had generations preceding them of grandparents, cousins, aunts, and uncles who had served up the ranks. Whatever the reason, they had someone who was waiting and depending on their success.

Jesus has similar expectations. He is your creator and the one holding the master plan for your destiny. No matter what circumstance or situation that brought you to Jesus in the first place, your relationship and walk with him was predestined before you were formed in the womb.

Jeremiah 29:1

For I know the thoughts that I think toward you, saith the Lord, thoughts of peace, and not of evil, to give you an expected end. Then shall ye call upon me, and ye shall go and pray unto me, and I will hearken unto you. And ye shall seek me, and find me, when ye shall search for me with all your heart. And I will be found of you, saith the Lord: and I will turn away your captivity, and I will gather you from all the nations, and from all the places whither I have driven you, saith the Lord; and I will bring you again into the place whence I caused you to be carried away captive.

Each day as it seemed like the number of people in our flight dwindled, I observed how the others stayed the course to overcome. There was one girl in my flight who had threatened suicide. She came from a family of high-ranking officers and was under a great amount of pressure to perform. There were others within our crew who had to stay self-motivated so that they could pass the fitness requirements.

During our second week of camp there was some kind of pestilence that affected one of the squadrons. Many people became sick and a few people died. For young people far away from home these things seemed devastating, and many were fearful. Jesus promised in the word that his plan for us is a righteous plan to bring us to an expected end.

In training each day there were obstacles, tests, inspections seemed like there was always something to overcome. We came back to the squadron each evening tired, worn, and dirty. Every day I wanted to quit. I wanted to give up. I approached each new day in faith, not knowing what the end would be. I didn't know If I would pass. I didn't know if I would make it through. However, I did know that I belonged to Jesus. I was in his hands. That relationship is worth fighting for no matter the circumstance, no matter what the situation, regardless of what you're going through or even what your natural eyes may see. Put on the whole armor of God and fight the good fight of faith! When you're going through trials and tests your gifts start to make room for the Lord to operate in your life. You learn to know them that labor among you.

You learn to trust your life in someone else's hand. That is the fear of the Lord, knowing that he allowed you to be put situations, not to trust in the flesh of man, but to trust in the Spirit of God.

The Lord has already declared prophetically that the battle is already won through Jesus Christ. We have been made victorious with Jesus by faith and through his Spirit. So, spiritually the warfare is already won. The Lord did all of the work for us on the cross. However, in the natural realm there is a process, a faith walk that must take place for us to see the manifestation of that end result in our life. The just shall live by faith. We walk by faith, not by sight. The Lord Jesus gave us our spiritual armor so that in our daily walk of obedience, when we put on the whole armor of God, we overcome the troubles and the trials by faith. As you are walking this daily walk with the Lord you learn to stand on your foundation of faith, and you learn to hear the voice of the Lord. When you're in boot camp and you have weapons, along with a mission to protect and serve there is still more required for you in your role as an effective member of the Body of Christ.

1 Cor 12:20

But now are they many members, yet one body.

So, not only do we learn how to operate in our calling as a member and how to utilize our gifts and talents for the uplifting of the Kingdom of God, but we learn to know those who labor among us, how to operate in unity and one accord, as well as being obedient to do and implement the will and purpose of the Lord Jesus in his timing. Though you are ordained to salvation before the foundations of the world were established, boot camp represents the establishment of a strong, solid foundation of faith in Jesus Christ.

Warfare is real! Take full advantage of your training so that you are thoroughly prepared. No one wants to start from square one again because they weren't strong enough to stick with it to the end. Remember that God will not put more on us than we can bare. He has fully equipped us for every situation we will encounter. Make a decision to stick with the Lord no matter what. The Lord wants to establish relationships with those who totally trust in Him and who are not willing to give up at the first hurdle. So, pick up your weapons and fight; stand firm on the foundation of faith you've been given.

NO STRIPES ALLOWED

Whosoever therefore shall humble himself as this little child, the same is the greatest in the kingdom of heaven.

At the start of boot camp, as well as most of the time you're in boot camp, your drill sergeant's main goal is to break you down. The men are weeded out from the boys and the women from the girls. Only the strong will survive! From the start, you are totally humbled. Regardless of what rank you signed up as or even what your goal rank is, while you're in training it doesn't matter. Throughout the time you are in training, you are addressed as trainee. Also, more importantly, you cannot think about having your stripes sewn onto your uniform. Everything that means anything is given to you upon the completion of your training.

The process is designed to humble you. You must rid yourself of old habits and old ways of thinking. For this reason, I believe the Lord requires us to come unto Him as little children. Children are teachable. They are not set in their ways. He is the potter, and we are the clay. He can easily shape and mold us into the vessels He has called us to be. Can you begin to see why I compare spiritual boot camp with my experience in the Us Air Force? If not yet, you will soon see!

After my first true week in the US Air Force, I must have overdosed on humble pie. I was a part of a rather large flight (training group), which started out with about thirty females. I do not know if it was taking a shower together with that many women that started the breaking down of my flesh, or if it was actually using the restroom in front of others that did it for me.

In the spiritual aspect, the Lord must have a humble vessel to use for the uplifting of his kingdom. There is no other way, for it is stated in His Word.

If my people, which are called by my name, shall humble themselves, and pray, and seek my face, and turn form their wicked ways; then will I hear from heaven, and will forgive their sin, and will heal their land.

2 Chron 7:14

So, with this being said, when your truly surrender yourself to Christ as a yielded vessel, you'd better believe you'll be humbled before going forth with what the Lord has called you to do in its fullness. Some things the Lord will allow so that you will absolutely be dependent upon Him and exercise undoubted faith.

There is one particular time in my life when I remember being humbled. It was when I first totally committed myself to the ministry, and I said, "For Jesus I live, and for Jesus I die. I'm taking up my cross, and I'm following after you, Lord." After this, I began experiencing trials that I could have never prepared myself for. My finances began to dwindle, my employment was in jeopardy, my two homes went into foreclosure, and the list can go on and on. Aside from being humbled, it was embarrassing. There was no way to explain to others I knew what was taking place in my life. From the outside looking in, with things happening one after another, people thought for sure I was suffering punishment from God from being outside of his will or something. No one could understand. I even had a radio show, and I always came on with, "Good Morning, and thanks for joining in with us as we are seeking God's face like never before." Any sarcastic person in the world would have said, "There is no way, with all that's going on with her, that she's seeking God's face. If she were, those things wouldn't be happening." Again, I say the humble way is the only way, and the difference between military boot camp and spiritual boot camp is that with the lord Jesus, you oftentimes have no idea when the training will be over. With the US Air Force, however, I knew I could count down the weeks…6,5,4,3,2,1. That's what makes it a faith walk.

One thing is for sure; after you have been humbled, you can look forward to being exalted by God. When he promotes you, you will be in a better position to receive what He has for you, and you will be better equipped to handle the trials and tribulations throughout daily spiritual warfare.

For whosoever exalteth himself shall be abased; and he that humbled himself shall be exalted. *Luke 14:11*

When I was introduced to Jesus Christ, I didn't know what to expect. At the time of our introduction, I was a wreck. I was a mess and certainly I was out of shape spiritually as well as naturally. My spiritual condition required the Lord Jesus' refining fire. I knew that what I was doing and what I had been doing wasn't working and I was sure that I didn't want any part of the world any longer. My heart was ready for Jesus Christ to come in and do the increase in my life.

The Beginning of Wisdom is the Fear of the Lord. Proverbs 9:10

Like the word says fear of the lord is only the beginning and it lines up with the humility the Lord desires of us. When I encountered the Lord Jesus in the Spirit for the first time, there was an immediate change in me spiritually. He mended my broken heart because my heart was healed, I was able to receive the love of Jesus completely. The heart is the source of life. It's what keeps you breathing. It is what keeps the blood flowing. When Jesus stepped in and took residence, then I was persuaded and encouraged I had been redeemed by the Blood of the Lamb and my life was no longer my own. He purchased me with his blood, and I had a predestined purpose in him.

To experience unity in the faith by his Spirit you must get to a place where you let go of self completely! You recognize quickly that this life in Christ is not about you at all. Everything you do is about doing the Lord's will and his purpose. You're not focused on your rank. You don't care about titles or stripes, you're focused on obedience. You want to fulfill your mission. You want to please your Savior and compel others to be reconciled to him. You want to learn his precepts. That requires humility. Put all other knowledge aside. He is not logical. This is a faith walk you know nothing except that Jesus Christ is the Alpha and the Omega. He is the First and the Last. He is the Beginning and the End... The Author and Finisher of your faith. When that concept is hid in your heart, then you're content with not having stripes because you don't want to be seen at all. However, you want Jesus to shine through you.

Galatians 2:19-20

For I through the law am dead to the law, that I might live unto God. I am crucified with Christ: nevertheless I live; yet not I, but Christ liveth in me: and the life which I now live in the flesh I live by the faith of the Son of God who loved me and gave himself for me.

We must understand that the main goal of boot camp is prepare us for spiritual warfare, battle. You must learn how to face the enemy. You need to know what to do and what not to do, learn what to say and what not to say. So as a quick footnote, I'd like to have you add to your memory bank that everything you encounter, you cannot always blame on the devil. The Lord may have you in a position because you're a "trainee." So, speak to your Commander (Jesus) on a regular basis so that you're on one accord regarding your training.

Much of this humility training is to get you to a place where you are after God's own heart. Your heart should be in sync with his, so that you and He are one in unity. The passionate pursuit of his righteousness and his glory must be mingled in the foundation of faith so that your works are not in vain. So, what are you waiting for? Your life is no longer your own. People are depending on your obedience! So, pick up your weapons and contend for the faith!

YOUR DIET CHANGES

The first week in boot camp will most likely seem like one of the longest weeks ever if you're truly seeking God as you should. Not only are you required to do a lot of work, but your diet changes. As the day goes on, you're given only certain options of food to eat. Certain unhealthy things have been cut from your diet. You've began to live a new life and therefore, you eat new things. Day by day, you begin to lose the taste for those things you used to eat. In the mess hall, we could only have water of Gatorade. No soda, No coffee, No energy drinks like Red Bull or Amp. Absolutely No sweets, candy, cakes, potato chips.... nothing! Spiritually it is the same way! The things you take in should be spiritually edifying.

He that hath an ear, let him hear what the Spirit of The Lords saith unto the churches; To him that overcometh will I give to eat of the tree of life, which is in the midst of the paradise of God.
Revelation 2:7

We begin to eat things that preserve life and show positive fruits. See, there's a saying, "The apple doesn't fall too far from the tree." So, with the true and living God being your father, you should show characteristics of Him, because you've accepted Him as your personal Lord and Savior and you have been made in His likeness.

Ho, everyone that thirsteth, come ye to the waters, and that hath no money; come ye buy and eat; ye come buy win and milk without money and without price. Wherefore do ye spend money for that which no bread? And you labour for that which satisfieth not? Hearken diligently unto me and eat ye that which is good and let your soul delight in the fatness.
Isaiah 55:1

Over a period of time, we begin to form good eating habits. We begin to hunger and thirst for those things that are conducive to a prosperous day on the battlefield for Christ. Oh, taste and see that the Lord is Good! Our diet has to change that we may eat the fat of the lamb.

Blessed are they which do hunger and thirst after righteousness for they shall be filled. *Matthew 5:6*

Take these scriptures in and hide them on the tablet of your heart. Be careful what you feed your spirit. This is one of the reasons why the Lord says for us to present ourselves living sacrifices, Holy and acceptable. The things that you are around and allow within your environment feed your spirit. The enemy is cunning, and oftentimes we can be caught unaware by the traps he has set up.

I used to love going bowling. It did not matter the time of day or night that I would go because all I wanted to do was bowl. However, now I must be careful of the time and know what's going on before I get there. Oftentimes, the bowling center has different events going on; one event in particular was glow bowling, where the lights are shut off, they play secular music, and even offer a place to drink and smoke. I cannot speak for everyone; however, in my experience, the music had familiar spirits with it. If I were to stay in an environment like that long enough, I would begin to reminisce on past times and think on the things that I used to do. I would even hear the song and begin to think on who I was in a relationship with at that time. Before you know it, you can get caught up in things that are not of God at all.

Certain things you watch on television can be negative food for your spirit. For instance, I was fascinated with the TV shows that promoted revenge and worldly justice. There is nothing wrong with those shows, you would think, from the outside looking in, but in my opinion, sitting and watching men sometimes get away with murder because of the law and so on would have me to be angry and frustrated. Those are demonic forces. It may seem like an innocent television show, but subconsciously things are placed within your spirit, and for me, it was anger. Demonic forces are real, and life is already difficult enough without self-infliction. So why subject yourself when you don't have to? Don't even open that door.

I'm not going to go into too much depth with this, but just as you can feed your spirit man, you can feed demonic forces surrounding you because you've been made subject by someone else and their "visiting" spirits. For instance, if you're a smoker, and you've been asking for deliverance from this spirit, but yet you continue to put yourself amongst smokers and continue to smoke, then you are feeding that spirit. If you have a lying spirit, and you've asked the Lord to deliver you from lying, but you continue to put yourself in situations where you have to lie, then you are feeding that spirit. If you're praying for deliverance from a lust or fornication spirit, and yet you continue to put yourself in a position to fall to the temptation of having pre-marital sex, then you're feeding that spirit, and it will continue to grow stronger not weaker. This is with anything. If you continue to feed something, it will strengthen. So, for this reason, always be aware of what you are feeding your spirit, knowing that your body is the temple where the Lord resides. Seek the face of God continuously and protect your anointing.

You may ask me, "What feeds the Spirit, Pastor?" Well, one of the core traits of my personality was to analyze things. Early in my spiritual walk I began to think on these things and ask the Lord certain questions like: "How do I seek for you? Not just seek You, but find You? I desire You, I long for you, and yet You are seemingly so far beyond my grasp!" These questions I asked often. So, I would indulge myself in the Word. Yes, it seems so simple, but when you are extremely hungry, it seems to take so long to get full. Even as I would read the Word my hunger would actually increase. I would hang on every word as if I were reading a love letter with the very hope of knowing the heart of God. I'm reminded of a scripture in James 4:8, which says to draw near unto God, and He will draw near to you. The more I ate, the hungrier I was. I wanted more wisdom, more knowledge, more understanding...more of His Spirit! It became an addiction. I found myself asking God, "How do I get more?"

But God hath revealed them to us by His Spirit: For the Spirit searcheth all things, yea, the deep things of God. For what man knoweth the things of a man, save the Spirit of man which is in him? Even so the things of God knoweth no man. But the Spirit of God.

I Corinthians 2:10-11

I had answered my own question. I needed to draw nearer to God. This required more action on my end. I couldn't just have an ordinary relationship. So, to satisfy my hunger for God I began to praise Him more. Faith moves God and the Word says He inhabits the praises of His people (Psalms 22:3). The more I praised God without wavering and without reservation, the more filled (I wasn't feeling so empty and void) I became. While this was pleasing my appetite naturally, the Lord fed me spiritually with new revelations through my praise. Even in the midst of my praise the Lord would reveal locations of my enemies as well as what my enemy's next plot was. Through that time period in my life I realized that the mind and heart of God are made known through His Spirit. With His Spirit comes great tasting fruit. The fruit is good to the last drop and extremely healthy. The fruits of the Spirit are love, joy, peace, longsuffering, gentleness, faith, meekness, and temperance (Galatians 5:22-23). Once you've been made new in Christ, then you understand that you're made in this image and likeness. So, then you will bring forth the same fruit (I speak more of this in later chapters). Ephesians 5:9 reminds us that the fruit of the Spirit is in all goodness and righteousness and truth. So, the fruits, too, are forms of armor which much be utilized daily to stay a step ahead of the enemy and fuel our soul so that we have the momentum to press toward the mark for the prize.

It kills the enemy to see us walking in love and showing it toward one another with gentleness and humility. Oftentimes, it's not what we say, but what we do. The fruits are characteristics which require action and following through. Kill your enemy with kindness. Utilize the joy of the Lord as your strength in battle. Notice I said joy and not happiness. Happiness in temporary; joy lasts a lifetime. Hold fast to your most holy foundation of faith knowing the victory is already won.

A successful start to your day on the battlefield would be to first acknowledge God in all your ways, for He will direct your paths (Proverbs 3:6). Put on your whole armor. You cannot leave home without it.

Every day throughout the day while I was in boot camp in the US Air Force, I can remember being checked or inspected from top to bottom. Our commanding officers and drill instructors were always looking for something wrong. They never missed a beat. If there was anything wrong with our uniform or if something was missing, not only were we required to fix the issue, but we were most times required to drop and do pushups or flutter kicks as a method of corrective action. On some occasions, I was made an example to the entire flight (group I was assigned to), and they also were required to do the push-ups as well for whatever my mistake was. So, it is important to go out with your whole armor because if you leave some part of your armor at home, you may wind up in a situation you're going to suffer consequences for, and your mistake can affect others around you who are in your inner circle like friends and family.

But seek ye first the kingdom of God, and His righteousness, all these all things shall be added unto you. Matthew 6:33

If you make God your main focus and you're seeking His face (Not his hand), you cannot go wrong. The old life has been passed away; all the things have been made new in Christ. Keep this in mind. I'll say it over and over again, faith cometh by hearing. You have a new walk, a new talk, a new diet, a whole new mission. You've now been served with orders to report to your position on the battlefield for Christ as a full-time soldier. Keep in mind that this is not your own turf; we're on foreign soil. We are in this world, but not of this world. Knowing that you are not on your own turf, you must consistently communicate with your commanding officer (Jesus Christ) for daily instruction and missions that must be accomplished.

When you surrender completely to the will and purpose of Christ, this is a lifestyle change. You have the heart of God and you have His Spirit within you. Because his spirit resides within you, it's His Spirit that craves the righteousness of God! You thirst for his Spirit and you hunger for the Bread of Life, the Word of God. As the Lord continues to pour His Spirit upon you; the refining fire that accompanies His Spirit begins to purify you. To do (accomplish) this, He brings all of the dirt and the filth of your old man to the surface to be cleansed of it. Your appetite that came with the old life is put away!

For some people this is a process, however, for some others there is an immediate deliverance that came with your repentance. He, through the Holy Spirit removed the taste of some things out of your mouth. Then you realize deliverance has encountered you.

The Spirit is Willing, but the Flesh is Weak.

It is imperative that we walk by the spirit to not fulfill the lust of the flesh.

Galatians 5:15-26

This I say then, walk in the Spirit, and ye shall not fulfil the lust of the flesh. For the flesh lusteth against the spirit, and the spirit against the flesh: and these are contrary the one to the other: so that ye cannot do the things that ye would. But if ye be led of the spirit, ye are not under the law. Now the works of the flesh are manifest, which are; adultery, fornication, uncleanness, lasciviousness, idolatry, witchcraft, hatred, variance, emulations, wrath, strife, seditions, heresies, envying, murders, drunkenness, revellings, and such like: of the which I tell you before, as I have also told you in time past, that they which do such things shall not inherit the Kingdom of God. But the Fruit of the Spirit is love, joy, peace, longsuffering, gentleness, goodness, faith, meekness, temperance: against such there is no law. And they that are Christ's have crucified the flesh with the affections and lusts. If we live in the spirit, let us also walk in the spirit. Let us not be desirous of vain glory, provoking one another, envying one another.

The old way of life was according to the things of the flesh, but the new man is spiritual and is renewed day by day. In walking by the Spirit, we sow into ourselves spiritual seeds of righteousness. In doing so we reap fruits of the Spirit which are pleasing in the sight of God. If we sow to the flesh, we shall reap carnal things. Be sure to put the flesh under subjection so that you are not distracted, but fruitful in going forth doing the Lord's business. Remember we are in this world but not of it. We have a mission to fulfill. Lives are depending on our obedience.

1 Cor 9: 24-27

Know ye not that they which run in a race run all, but one receiveth the prize? So, run, that ye may obtain. And every man that striveth for the mastery is temperate in all things. Now they do it to obtain a corruptible crown, but we an incorruptible. I therefore so run, not as uncertainly, so fight I, not as one that beateth the air. But I keep under my body and bring it unto subjection: lest that by any means, when I have preached to others, I myself should be a castaway.

Just as it is in the military today, while at war, all of your daily needs will be met for you to accomplish the missions which you are given in the midst of warfare. You are provided with your weapons. You're provided with the ability to effectively communicate, and you are given food and all other immediate needs to operate successfully. So, also will your Heavenly Father provide you with all the things that you need to carry out His will and purpose in your life.

The mission is to do the Lord's will and do his purpose. He is our exceedingly great reward. We are building the Kingdom of God with the ultimate goal of residing on high with the Lord. We are the Bride, His Church. So, let his Holy Spirit do a work in you so he can reign completely. Put on the whole armor of God building up your most holy faith and go on unto perfection in him.

EXERCISE (TRIALS AND TRIBULATIONS)

Every morning throughout my time in basic training when I served in the US Air Force, reveille awoke us throughout the week at 0430 hours. We were allotted a certain amount of time to brush our teeth, make our bed, and to fall out for PT (Physical Training). In the beginning, it was extremely hard. I was not in the shape that I originally thought I was in, but as I continued day after day, I became used to the process, exercising became easier, and the conditioning actually worked.

I consider exercise in that aspect to be of comparison to our daily trials and tribulations in a sense. Tests and trials come to make us strong. They are form of conditioning. They help build endurance. For the race is not given to swift or the battle to the strong, but those who endure to the end shall be saved.

That the trial of your faith, being much more precious than of gold that perisheth, though it be tried with fire, might be found unto praise and honor and glory at the appearing of Jesus Christ.   1 Peter 1:7

Daily trials and tribulations are for faith purposes. For it is indeed impossible to please God without faith. Especially, in these last and evil days. Trials work patience. The Lord is our Goldsmith. He always knows just the right temperature the Gold needs in order to be refined and made into something beautiful and worth using.

And not only so, but we glory in tribulations also knowing that tribulation worketh patience, and patience, experience, and experience, hope. Rom 5:4

So, just as we did in military, as we exercised daily, we built tolerance, stamina, patience, strength, and endurance. The same is also in our daily trials and tribulations throughout our spiritual warfare. So, lift up ye heads O' ye gates. Pick up your weapons and fight!

It is ok to have cravings too, especially when you're put on a strict diet! This is natural. Personally, I craved a close relationship. I still do. I often asked the who, what, when, where, and how questions. I needed to know Jesus on an intimate level. I wanted my heart to beat in sync with my commander, so we were on one accord at all times. I knew he died for me, but what was my purpose? Why did I have to be a pastor? Why was I trusted with so great a task? Why was the war so hard to fight? When will this all be over? Where will I end up after all of this?

So many questions were going through my mind just as they did in my first few weeks of basic training. How I would be able to contribute to this mission effectively, was one. Through all of this I was beginning to fall in love with Jesus. I developed a trust like no other. He put me in a position where I knew without a doubt my commander and drill sergeant could do all things but fail and that His training was the best training.

Spiritual boot camp lasts much longer than six weeks as I mentioned earlier. I can reflect on one of my first major trials, which I considered to be warfare or OJT, if you will. The Lord wanted me to put all of my faith and trust in Him, to know that through every trial is a promotion. So, I was on the potter's wheel, and I couldn't move. He told me to separate from my family. This task right out of the gate was one of the hardest things I ever had to do. I am the oldest of six children, the bottom three being very young. It hurt my heart, and I had no understanding. I began to think, "What a way to start boot camp; change my diet and add a cup of obedience to go along with it."

The Lord gave me the Genesis 12:1 scripture to support His method of training. My family did not take the separation well at all. First, they did not believe that I was called by God for anything, let alone being a pastor. Then some believed that if God loved me so much then He would not instruct me to do such a thing. I didn't believe it would have hurt so much if they weren't Holy Ghost filled believers. I thought, "Couldn't they go into intercessory prayer to confirm this? Surely, God would tell them I'm being torn down for His Glory. Of course not, that would be too much like right!"

So, at that point I became totally isolated. Just as it is in the natural world, so it is also in the spirit. When I went away to San Antonio, Texas, to start boot camp training I felt the same way—completely isolated. There was no one I could communicate with or relate to. I was simply left to face the time. I initially wanted to write home to tell my family of my progress and all of the new things I was learning, then over time the urge dwindled away.

Another thing I could remember within the first few weeks of boot camp was the psychology tests. They wanted to be sure our mind was right. We needed to prove ourselves stable and able to handle wartime conditions. So, we went through a series of tests. These tests asked several of the same questions over and over, but they were phrased differently each time to prevent a programmed answer.

Our spiritual boot camp is the same way. Without me being able to communicate with my family the way I wanted to initially, I thought I would go crazy. However, the Lord used mu time of isolation in order for me to draw near unto Him and to learn of His operations and His administrations of the Spirit. He had to "show me the ropes." I had to be strengthened in Him. The Lord taught me about what my purpose was as well as shared his overall vision, mission, goals, and the role I would play (His expectations of me as a soldier). The more He shared with me, the more inclined my eyes were to see what He was willing to show me, and my ears were inclined to hear His voice and the instruction he set forth.

Through all of this, my first reaction while being "in the flesh" was to be angry with my family. They talked about my husband and me like we were dogs. They thought that we were clueless and confused about truly hearing the voice of God. That's why I thank God that He said, "His sheep hear His voice." The more I would seek God, the more jacked up my family became. Things started to become clearer as I was on the outside looking in. People who I thought were on my side really weren't for me at all. I believe that is why The Lord reminds us in the Word that we must choose a side. You are either for me or against me. There is no grey area. Nevertheless, my family that I thought had my best interest at heart really didn't care at all. However, it took sanctification and obedience to see things with a spiritual eye. I was in the valley, the wilderness, and there was no end in sight.

What I began to slowly understand is that no one else can fight this good fight of faith for you. No one can run your race, but you. No matter how much I wanted to sit and explain to my family what the Lord was doing, my mouth was shut for a season regarding this. The last thing I wanted to do was to put my feet in something that the Lord told me was hands off. I had to let go and follow the orders I was given, without deviating. There were times when I felt like Joseph, and no matter what the end of the story was, the hard part was living through it and coming to that expected end.

The psychology of it all played a huge role in my training. My mind was always going. It was somewhat similar to a chess game. I thought of the consequences of my every move. There was no room for error. When training for warfare, every move must be calculated. You must know the mind of your commander as well as the mind of your enemy. The decisions you make cannot be based on emotion. They must be rational and thorough.

I needed to keep that statement in mind that every time I wanted to go home to my family. No emotion, be strong in the Lord, encourage yourself. I had to recite these things in my mind often, especially since my personality with regard to my family is that I've always strived for their approval, subconsciously. Deep in the very bottom of my heart I didn't care about the negativity they showed toward me, because my Love overshadowed that.

The heat of this trial season with family seemed nearly unbearable. Nevertheless, I knew the Lord, my commander knew what He was doing. All things work together for the good. Where there is unity, there is strength. So, as long as my heart and mind were on one accord with the Lord, then I was assured that together we could be proactive and penetrate the enemy's line of fire; eliminating his tactics in every shape, fashion, form, and dimension; rendering him powerless and ineffective.

Ecc 9:11

... Race is not given to the swift, nor battle to the strong, but those who endure to the end shall be saved.

First, let's get to the heart of the matter. The Lord allows tests, circumstances, and situations to make room for the operations of his Spirit. The word stated that we plant, others may water, but God only gives the increase. We must wait on the Lord to move in our lives by doing so we see the manifestation of signs, miracles, and wonders that accomplish the increasing of our faith. While growing in leaps and bounds we see the Lord glorified in us. When you're saved by grace and you're contending for the faith on the battlefield the very foundation of your relationship is going to be tested. Will you come out pure as gold?

No one wants to go through hardship. We do not want any trouble. However, the trials keep you fit for the race we're in called life. How can you endure to the end if you are not spiritually fit for the battle that you're to encounter? Each trial and the overcoming power given by the faith strengthens our relationship with Jesus Christ, builds character and testimonies which compel others to choose Jesus Christ as their Savior just as well.

With any job there are seasoning requirements. You're not going to feel like you're on the mountain all the time. You'll most likely feel like you're often in the valley, but wherever you are, you must know that Jesus is there. Everything you're doing, you're doing it side by side with him. This is a distance run. This is not a sprint and there are no short cuts. One will chase a thousand. So, again I say that many peoples' lives and their ability to overcome is greatly dependent upon your obedience and the power of your personal testimony of faith.

When you're going through a circumstance or situation where your faith is being tested you always want to know when it's going to end. Why am I going through this? What is the Lord trying to show me? He is God. He is your creator. He is the one with the plan. This is the fear of the Lord. You're in his hands. Of Course, there are vulnerabilities, but as his church, we must stand as the weaker vessel.

1 Peter 3:7

Likewise, ye husbands, dwell with them according to knowledge, giving honour unto the wife, as unto the weaker vessel, and as being heirs together of the grace of life, that your prayers be not hindered.

So, this is a spiritual life, a spiritual walk with the Lord and spiritually he is the Bridegroom. With him as the head we must trust him to cover his Bride and lead her in the right direction. Give the Lord your weakness, so that his strength will be made perfect in the midst of it. With each trial you encounter, there is a revelation of Jesus Christ. You learn his names. You learn that he is a Redeemer, a Father. He is a Healer. He is a Refuge. You can always go to him. He is a Provider. He is a Light in the midst of darkness. When you allow the Potter to shape you on that potter's wheel it hurts and is often very uncomfortable. He teaches you discipline, the fear of the Lord, with that fear you learn to trust.

Rom 5:1-5

Therefore, being justified by faith, we have peace with God through our Lord Jesus Christ: by whom also we have access by faith into grace wherein we stand and rejoice in hope of the glory of God. And not only so, but we glory in tribulations also: knowing that tribulation worketh patience; and patience, experience; and experience, hope: and hope maketh not ashamed; because the Love of God is shed abroad in our hearts by the Holy Ghost which is given unto us.

The word to focus on in the mentioned scripture is experience. Through the experience is the birth of hope and the love of Christ is strengthened that much more within you. To endure to the end, you must love Jesus Christ. You must love being his Servant. You must desire to be in unity with him by his Spirit. Besides the Lord allowing tests and trials for you to build a strong relationship with him, He wants to have you stand on your most holy faith. These trials prepare you for battle, that you will stand against the wiles of the devil. He prepares you to quench the fiery darts of the wicked and to stand in the evil day. In previous chapters, we discussed how there were many reasons why men and women joined the military. They had their reasons. However, with Jesus Christ there is a predestination. You are called and He qualifies you.

John 6:44

No man can come to me, except the Father which hath sent me draw him: and I will raise him up at the last day.

      Knowing these things, the trials are to bring you to your expected end in Jesus Christ. Just as with our natural military, when you enlist or join, you have a role to abide in.

      You are given a field of duty or mission of service. Just as well with the Lord Jesus. You have a mission to fulfill in him, a place as a member of the Body of Christ. To be effective and efficient in such a role there is training. Most training for missions concerning spiritual warfare are not the kind that can be taught in word only, but in the demonstration of the power of the Holy Ghost. Some in the military would call it OJT (On The Job Training). You must go through it. Therein is the testimony of the Lord Jesus Christ established from faith to faith and glory to glory.

1 Cor 2:4-5

And my speech and my preaching was not with enticing words of man's wisdom, but in the demonstration of the Spirit and of power: that your faith should not stand in the wisdom of men, but in the power Of God.

You are needed on the battlefield soldier. Get off the sidelines and fight the good fight of faith!

KNOW YOUR ENEMY

For we wrestle not against flesh and blood, but against principalities, against powers, against the rulers of the darkness of this world, spiritual wickedness in high places.

Ephesians 6:12

We're in spiritual war, and our enemy does not rest. He knows us better that we know ourselves. We must look at the people as spiritual beings and not look at them at face value. For it is not the flesh that we focus on, but the spiritual principality behind the flesh. Our enemy knows our strengths as well as our weaknesses. He doesn't forget them but uses them against us. However, we must also understand that "No weapon formed against thee shall prosper" (Isaiah 54:17). In Romans 8:37, The Lord gives us confirmation that the battle is already won. "Nay, in all these things we are more than conquerors through Him that loved us."

And there was a war in heaven: Michael and his angels fought against the dragon; and the dragon fought and his angels,
And prevailed not, neither was their place found anymore in heaven.
And the great dragon was cast out, that old serpent, called the devil, and Satan, which deceiveth the whole world: he was cast out into the earth, and his angels were cast out with him.
And I hear a loud voice saying in heaven, now is come salvation, and strength, and the kingdom of our God, and the power of his Christ; for the accuser of our brethren is cast down, which accused them before our God day and night.

Rev 12:7-10

When you are at war, you must know who your enemy is and what his devices are against you. Know what his tactics are. Know exactly what you are fighting for and stand firm on your belief, do not waver. So, this scripture tells us that we are fighting for salvation, strength, and the kingdom of our God. It is confirmed that the battle is won; the enemy shall not prevail.

Moreover, the word of the Lord came unto me saying,
Son of Man take up a lamentation upon the king of Tyrus, and say unto him, thus saith the Lord God; thou sealest up the sum, full of wisdom, and perfect in beauty.
Those hast been in Eden the garden of God; every precious stone was thy covering, the sardius, the topaz, and the diamond, the beryl, the onyx, and the

jasper, the sapphire, the emerald, and the carbuncle, and gold: the workmanship of thy tabrets and of thy pipes was prepared in thee in the day that thou wast created.
Thou art the anointed cherub that covereth, and I have set thee so: thou wast upon the holy mountain of God; thou hast walked up and down in the midst of the stones of fire.
Thou wast perfect in thy ways from the day that thou was created, till iniquity was found in thee.
By the multitude of thy merchandise they have filled the midst of thee with violence, and thou hast sinned: therefore I will cast thee as profane out of the mountain of God: and I will destroy thee O covering cherub from the midst of the stones of fire.
Thine heart was lifted up because of thy beauty, thou hast corrupted thy wisdom by reason of thy brightness, I will cast thee to the ground, I will lay thee before kings, that they behold thee.   *Ezekiel 28:11-17*

Knowing the history of your enemy is extremely important. If someone were hateful toward you, wouldn't you want to know why? Oftentimes, when I realize that I may have offended someone, I trace my steps back and ask myself, "What did I do?" Well, the Bible also tells us that many of His people are destroyed because of lack of knowledge. So, we must set out to know the deep things of God.

We need to know who our enemy is. He is jealous because the Lord has come that we may have life and have it more abundantly. He is jealous of our favor and what the Lord has promised us. The Word of God reassures us that eye hath no seen, nor hath ear heard, nor entereth the heart of man the things which He hath prepared for them that love him (1 Corinthians 2:9, paraphrased). In John 14:2, the Lord says, "In my father's house are many mansions: if it were not so, I would have told you. I go to prepare a place for you."

So, the Lord has promised everlasting life to those that believe in Him, but the time of our enemy is short, ending with him being thrown into the lake of fire. I believe this is also why the Lord says to us in 1 John 3:13, "Marvel not, my brethren, if the world hate you." The world hated you because you are not of this world. The Word tells us that if we are His children then we would act like our Father. The world belongs to the Prince of Darkness. Satan is the ruler of this world, and we are hated because we are now joint heirs with Jesus Christ by His Spirit. We have been made in His image, given His power, authority, and inheritance, which the enemy is no longer privy to.

In a natural military perspective, I can make an example of the wars which were fought overseas. Initially, when our troops were sent to fight and to rebuild, there was a great resistance. Some of the citizens and the foreign governments hated us for coming in and trying to restructure and set order. When people don't have common beliefs, things become an absolute mess. Again, I must remind you that everything is spiritual. People are willing to die for what they believe.

Our situation regarding spiritual warfare is no different. We must be willing to die for our mission. We are here to win souls for Christ. Things must be set in order before Christ returns for His people. This will indeed cause people to hate you. As a soldier for Christ we must call our sin for what it is. Exposing sin and telling people to repent for the kingdom of God is at hand is bold, offensive, and will cause the enemy to open fire. However, we cannot be concerned with the faces, as Jeremiah reminds us. We must recognize the spirit behind the face as a potential enemy and threat and should be treated as such.

Previously, I made mention of how the Lord had separated me from my family for a season. Well, one situation that I faced and overcame as a teenager was sexual abuse. Once I told my mother what had taken place, I was rather disappointed with her response. From an analytic perspective I tried to look at things from all viewpoints. After attempting to pull things apart, nothing seemed to make sense. I was raped and molested by my stepfather, but my mother chose to stay with him. No matter how many times I revisited the issue it didn't make sense. This is when the Lord told me to separate. Sometimes we can be so close to a situation that we cannot see the full inner workings of the enemy until we step back and look from the outside in.

Once the enemy knows that you're a child of God and that he cannot have your soul, he will try to devour the very presence of God in you. After all that I had been through, I had no desire to fight. I didn't know how to fight. I was seemingly in a war all by myself. However, though the enemy penetrated my inner ranks and put me in a position to surrender my spiritual weapons, somehow my commander had a backup plan. His plan is always the best plan. In spiritual battle we are entrusted with the Lord's Word and His gifts and yet we decide not to always abide by the orders set. We can't be consumed with that. We must seek out our own salvation with fear and trembling. We must concentrate on being obedient to what the Lord says and when we've done all that we can do, stand and see the salvation of the Lord.

Though the situation with my stepfather may have hurt me, The Lord preserved my mind and my soul. Spiritual warfare has no age restriction. Just as the Lord states that before we were created in the womb, He knew us; the enemy, too, had a plan to destroy and eliminate all useful soldiers.

Growing up, the enemy put all sorts of lies in my head. He had me believing that I wasn't worth loving. I felt that my mother didn't love me either and that she allowed it to happen to me. It seemed as if she chose him over me. The enemy said that was confirmation that she never loved me.

The time that I could have spent seeking God, I spent being angry with myself for not being good enough. A great bit of my teenage and young adult life I was inactive on the battlefield for Christ because I didn't know who I was in Christ and what power and authority I did have. I spent time trying to get the approval of "the world," not knowing that no matter what, "the world" can't and will never love me.

A major strategic tactic that enemies utilize in warfare is deception. When Jesus Christ walked the earth with his disciples, they asked the Lord what shall be the sign of thy coming be and the end of the world? (Matthew 24:3) The first thing the Lord Jesus shared in his response was that we take heed that no man deceives us. Deception plays a major role in spiritual warfare. The enemy will use tactics of deception to make you think you don't have what you do have. He will also come to make you think you don't know what you do know. So, if he can make you think the Lord Jesus is not with you, when in fact, he is with you, how much damage would that cause psychologically for you to go forth with confidence to do the will and purpose of Christ?

Luke 10:18-20

And he said unto them, I behold Satan as lighting fall from heaven. Behold, I give unto you the power to tread on serpents and scorpions, and over all the power of the enemy: and nothing shall by any mean hurt you. Notwithstanding in this rejoice not, that the sprits are subject unto you; but rather rejoice, because your names are written in heaven.

The enemy is well aware of what power and authority you have. If he could destroy it, he would. If he could steal it, he would because he has none. Because we have power and authority to overcome the enemy and his demonic forces he will come with false signs and wonders to attempt to get you to think you don't have what you do. When we walk in boldness and confidence by the spirit of faith the enemy trembles. He trembles that much more when you go forth together in unity by the Holy Spirit. Stand tall on your foundation of faith and obedience. When you've got a strong relationship with Jesus Christ, then the enemy will attempt to deceive you into believing you're weak in the faith. When you're moving forth in the power of God to fulfil your mission in Christ, then the enemy will attempt to make you think you don't have enough of the Holy Spirit to do his will and to do his purpose. As if you're not able to heal, as if you're not able to be used to set someone free, and as if you're not able to get a prayer through to the Most High, when in fact all things are possible through Jesus Christ who strengthens us.

Try The Spirit To Know

1 John 4:1

Beloved, believe not every spirit, but try the spirits whether they are of God: because many false prophets are gone out into the world.

2 Cor 11:13-15

For such are false apostles, deceitful workers, transforming themselves in the apostles of Christ. And no marvel; for Satan himself is transformed into an angel of light. Therefore, it is no great thing if his ministers also be transformed as the ministers of righteousness; whose end shall be according to their works.

Don't be deceived by them who creep in presenting themselves as brethren attempting to get you to compromise your faith. Jesus is not the author of confusion and he stated to us that we shall know them by their fruits. We must be spiritually sensitive to recognize the moving of the Holy Spirit within us and within certain situations and circumstances. You know Jesus Christ, your Savior. You know your God. You know his Word. You know he is real in you. You know he is the truth, the way, and the life. Jesus promised you he would never leave you neither forsake you. So, when the deceiver comes attempting to convince you that you don't have what you need to make it, know that he is a liar and has been from the beginning. Seek the Lord Jesus Christ for his Holy Spirit while he is yet available. He will keep you. He will comfort you. He will counsel you and guide you in the paths of all truths and righteousness.

Don't allow the enemy to deceive you into believing that the Lord isn't with you or that Holy Spirit within you in not enough to accomplish the will and purpose of the Most High. Do not allow deception to have you compromise by taking down for the enemy. Meaning, you must walk by faith and not by sight. You must utilize your gifts for the building of the Kingdom of God and tearing the Kingdom of Satan down. You must use your authority to do a greater works for the Lord Jesus meaning, signs, miracles, and wonders shall follow those that believe.

Galatians 2:4

And that because of false brethren unawares brought in, who came in privily to spy out our liberty which we have in Christ Jesus, that they might bring us into bondage.

Know who you are in Christ. Stand tall in him, believing only, knowing that no matter the circumstance or situation, he is your refuge. He is your strength. The enemy will attempt to convince you otherwise. You will encounter false brethren who have been sent to spy your liberties in Christ in the hope of finding some way to gain access to your weakness that they might bring you into bondage. If these enemies of the cross bring you into bondage, then how effective would you be on the battlefield for Christ? How much more diligent would you be in walking in your calling? Would you be effectively used to compel someone to surrender to the will and purpose of Christ? Could you be used to deliver someone, when you're in need of deliverance yourself? How effective to the mission is a prisoner of war?

Guard your heart. Guard your anointing. Be an effective gatekeeper. Hide in the Spirit of Holiness. Trust in the Lord with your whole heart. Speak the word of God throughout all circumstances and situations. Pray without doubting that Jesus will do what he said he will do even as we fulfil our obedience to his will and his purpose.

Understand that even if the enemy attempts to delay you or create stumbling blocks, he is still doing his job. Time is running out, and we cannot get time back. That's why the Lord urges us that we must fight while it's day because when night comes no man can work. Know who you are and what power you have. Recognize who your enemies are; no matter how close they may seem to be. Sound the alarm! This war is spiritual, and the enemy will use anyone he can to get the job done. So, what are you waiting for? Pick up your weapons and fight!

EQUIP YOURSELF WITH THE WHOLE ARMOR

Put on the whole armour of God, that ye may be able to stand against the whiles of the devil.

Stand therefore, having your loin girt about with the truth, and having on the breastplate of righteousness;

And your feet shod with the preparation of the gospel of peace;

Above all, taking the shield of faith, wherewith ye shall be able to quench the fiery darts of the wicked.

And take the helmet of salvation, and the sword of the Spirit, which is the word of God: praying always with all prayer and supplication in the Spirit, and watching thereunto with all perseverance and supplication for all saints;
Eph 6:11-14

For the weapons of our warfare are not carnal, but mighty through God to the pulling down of strongholds.   *2 Corinthians 10:4*

    Though the Lord has given us our basic weapons of warfare, which are listed in Ephesians chapter six, there are other means He has blessed us with as well for us to succeed in battle. However, our efficiency with the basics is extremely important to master before increasing the weapons in our arsenal.

    Some other weapons that we have access to include: the power of the Holy Ghost, praise and worship, and even our obedience, which will be discussed in later chapters. Being that we are predestined to fight as soldiers in the Lord's army, the Lord has been sure to provide us with all the weaponry and ammunition we need to fight a victorious battle.

Having Your Loins Girt About With Truth…

But the hour cometh and now is, when the true worshippers shall worship in Spirit and in truth: for the Father seeketh such to worship Him.

God is a Spirit and they that worship Him must worship Him in Spirit and in truth.   *John 4:23-24*

The Lord Jesus Christ states that He is the way, the truth, and the life (John 14:6, paraphrased). So, in the above scripture the Lord stated that the very first piece of spiritual armor He has given unto us was the truth, and the truth shall indeed set us free. Through our daily walk with Christ, we must not only be true to ourselves, we must be true to God as well. For the Lord sees all and He knows all. He already knows our heart and our mind and is a revealer of secrets.

There are things that many of us will need deliverance from, whether it be from drugs, alcohol, adultery, whatever the case may be, now is the time to be truthful to the Holy Spirit and give it to God. We have enough issues with the enemy as it is. We don't need any other baggage hindering us on the battlefield. If you know of these things, then the Lord knows them, and the enemy knows them. So, start with honesty.

David makes petitions to the Lord in Psalms 51:10: "Create in me a clean heart, O' God and renew a right spirit within me." Again, in Hebrews 4:16, the Lord welcomes us, "Let us therefore come boldly to the throne of grace, that we may obtain mercy, and find grace to help in the time of need." By doing so, we eliminate many of the fiery darts that the enemy will use against us.

Luke 9:35

And there came a voice out of the cloud, saying, this is my beloved son: hear him.

When you're going forth in the faith it's often somewhat easy to say to yourself, "I know the truth." Because He's someone you already have been given by the Holy Spirit. Sometimes, we don't allow the meaning to really marinade in our being. When Jesus Christ walked the earth, God the Father gave a command with his voice directly in the midst of the disciples giving them confirmation that Jesus Christ was his son and urged them to hear him.

Rom 10:17
So, then faith cometh by hearing, and hearing by the Word of God.

Jesus Christ is faith. He is the truth. When we are in a spiritual battle, we must hear the voice of truth in order to overcome the fiery darts of the enemy. Though we may know the voice of the Lord God, when you're in a situation or circumstance sometimes the enemy's voice is louder than the voice of truth. When you're in the midst of a trial, the voice of truth comes to edify and build up your Spirit man. He says, "I am with you," in a still, small voice. He says, "I love you; I will never leave you or forsake you."

Some instances you may only hear the Lord speak on few occasions for the sake of building trust. Yet, while going through that same situation that enemy pumps out lies in your ears like a machine gun. Those are those fiery darts. The enemy will use what you hear and see to show a lie. He will say, "look at what you've done. No one wants you. No one wants to be around you. You're a failure. You're worthless. You won't pass the test. Jesus doesn't want you anymore. He won't hear your prayer. What you're doing is pointless. Give up. Throw in the towel…" He is relentless.

That enemy no matter what shape, fashion, or form will attempt to feed you lies as long as you entertain them. Speak the truth to your situation. Resist the Devil and he will flee. We walk by faith and not by sight. The situations you're presented with in the natural will almost always seem impossible to man. Yet with Jesus Christ all things are possible to them that believe. Know the voice of truth. His sheep know his voice and will not follow after a stranger.

Nowhere To Run Nowhere To Hide

1 Kings 19:11-13

And he said, go forth, and stand upon the mount before the Lord. And behold, the Lord passed by, and a great and strong wind rent the mountains, and brake in pieces the rocks before the Lord; but the Lord was not in the win: and after the win and earthquake: and after the earthquake a fire; but the Lord was not in the fire: and after the fire a still, small voice and it was so, when Elijah heard it that he wrapped his face in his mantle, and went out, and stood in the entering in of the cave and behold, there came a voice unto him, and said, what doest thou here Elijah?

We have seen through the testimony of Jonah and through the testimony of the Prophet Elijah that you cannot run from the voice of God. You cannot hide from the Spirit of Truth. There is nowhere to run and there is nowhere to hide from His Spirit.

You cannot run from your calling. No matter how terrible the situation or matter may seem. You must obey the voice of the Lord one way or another the truth will find you out. No matter what we see in this earth, we are still called to do a work. He who began a good work in you will perform it until the day of Jesus Christ. The earth will continue to go this way, and continue to get more wicked, but regardless there is still a mission to fulfil for the time allotted.

Elijah was a prophet of the Lord chosen for a work in a time when the head of the Lord's people were corrupt. There were wars, famine, and the majority of the people were backslidden in sin. They did not want to walk in the truth and had commanded that the prophets of the Most High be slain. Though it seemed in that natural sense that there wasn't much work being done in the name of the Lord, spiritually the Spirit of the Lord was with his people. The Lord God is the same yesterday, today, and evermore.

Regardless of your present situation, you must face the truth and walk in the truth. The Lord is with those that believe. He will never leave thee nor forsake thee that you can boldly say He is your keeper and a present help in the time of trouble. We, who are the Children of God expose the lies of the enemy and maintain accountability within the House of God. We are faithful stewards of the Truth with our words as well as our deeds. The word tells us that in Christ there is the light and in him there is no darkness at all.

The Prophet Elijah ran into a cave. The Spirit of God did not lead him there. While in this cave full of darkness and fear, the Lord asked him, "Why are you here?" There is no fear in the truth. Perfect love casts out all fear. The Lord commanded him to come out of that dark place and stand on the mount. It was there the Lord was able to show him the power of God. He brought forth the wind, an earthquake, and the fire to build the confidence of his servant. We are lights that cannot be hid and we must go forth in that truth.

Hear the truth. Love the truth. Obey the truth. Hide the truth in your heart that you may not sin against him. The truth is what sets captives free.

1 John 4:6

We are of God: he that knoweth God heareth us; he that is not of God heareth not us. Hereby know we the Spirit of Truth, and the Spirit of Error.

This scripture is so relevant, especially in these last and evil days. When the Lord Jesus is purifying you through day to day warfare you will find that your spiritual being just wants true fellowship. You desire people who don't care about all of the formalities. You want what's real. You want the true believers in your inner circle with real encouragement who you can trust to get a prayer through. Some people, as much as you want them to, they just won't get it. They won't understand. No matter how much you speak the truth. No matter how many times. The world will not receive you. The world will not receive the truth, it falls on deaf ears. It doesn't make sense. They are tares amongst the wheat. You will know the difference. So, be not weary in well doing. You shall reap if you faint not.

Having On The Breastplate Of Righteousness...

But seek ye first the Kingdom of God, and His righteousness: and all these things shall be added unto you.   Matthew 6:34

Plainly, in this particular scripture, the Lord lets us know that we should first seek the kingdom of God and His righteousness. Take notice that it stated, "His righteousness", and not what our belief of what right is. This reminds me of a scripture in Proverbs 14:12, which states:

There is a way that seemeth right unto a man, but the end thereof are the ways of death (destruction).

Take note and recognize that our breastplate of righteousness is located just over our heart. The irony is our heart needs to be right. Righteousness is a major part of our spiritual weaponry. If we go anywhere without it, it leaves us open to the fiery darts of the enemy our heart has no protection or guard in front of it. Just visualize a police officer without a bulletproof vest. Well, the same goes for us as soldiers. If we are missing our breastplate of righteousness, we can be seriously wounded and even die from injuries that could have been prevented. Paul reminds us in Romans: "There is none righteous, no not one."

The Lord states in John 5:16, "The effective fervent prayer of a righteous man availeth much." Prayer is another one of our spiritual weapons, which I will discuss in more detail later chapters in this book, but the point is that in order to really get a prayer through expeditiously, you must be righteous. We must die daily to the flesh. We must repent, also saying, "Lord, have me decrease that you might increase. Have my will conform to yours, O' God, my Strength and Redeemer." We must ask ourselves, "Is this right in the sight of God?" At the end of the day, all we have is our righteousness and integrity.

There was a situation that the Lord allowed me to be in at one point in my life. I began going to a church where the people loved to praise God. When I first got there, I was so excited because I didn't have to praise God alone. I began to attend services on a regular basis and noticed things in operation which were contrary to the Word of God. Pretty soon, the apostle of the church became upset with the fact my husband and I refused to conform to the way they operated. The apostle began to pray for our demise. However, it was only because of our true heart and righteousness before God that we were not consumed. They literally wanted us dead, and the apostle who was also head pastor of the church indeed had the power to carry out her wishes in the spiritual realm, but when motives contradict the Word of God, the Lord simply will not allow it. My God's Word says, "Touch not my anointed and do my Prophet no harm." (Psalms 105:15). The righteous shall be lifted above the wicked and the workers of iniquity. The lesson learned in that situation is that the righteous in Christ are always victorious. I also learned that all things that seem Holy, look Holy, and act Holy outwardly are not necessarily so. In this day and age, it can be extremely hard to tell; but my Bible tells me that you will know them by their fruits. This is another prime example why you should be suited in the whole armor so you're not to be caught unaware.

I will greatly rejoice in the Lord, my soul shall be joyful in my God: for hath clothed me with the garments of salvation, he hath covered me with the robe of righteousness...   *Isaiah 61:10*

       Take note that righteousness is a part of your daily attire. This is a part of our uniform. Imagine policemen running out in the middle of an intersection to direct traffic without his uniform on. I do not believe he would get much accomplished without it. If anything, he would nearly ger run over! See, he would still have his title, but who could recognize him?

       The same goes for us Christians as well. We can have the title all day long, but we lose authority and respect if we do not also dress the part. Anyone who once served in the military reading this book my agree that you can recognize an officer in the military usually by the stitching on his lapel or on a hat. Our responsibility as a fellow soldier would be to salute the officer out of respect as we passed by. However, if I happen to walk past that officer who happens to be wearing civilian clothing, I will fail to salute the officer and allot him or her the respect they deserve because I would have no indication of who they might be. I would have no idea of their power, strength, authority, or ability.

Romans 3:10

As it is written, there is none righteous no not one.

       We must put on righteousness. By faith in Jesus Christ we are made righteous. He is our righteousness. To know the Lord is to know that righteousness is only obtained by faith in the son, Lord Jesus Christ. In our daily walk of faith, we must recognize that there is nothing that we can do to be righteous in the sight of God besides believing in him. This is a crucial part of our spiritual battles. You must know that Jesus Christ is your righteousness. The enemy will attempt to convince otherwise.

Rom 10:3-4

For they being ignorant of God's righteousness, and going about to establish their own righteousness, have not submitted themselves unto the righteousness of God.

For Christ is the end of the law for righteousness to everyone that believeth.

It is impossible to please the Lord without faith and there is no other work that can stand in the place of the works of faith. Contrary to popular belief we cannot go forth establishing our own righteousness. Because of these things we, as Children of God, have provoked the Lord to wrath. He has given us to sow, and to water. Yet, he alone giveth the increase. In all of our righteousness, we are yet filthy as rags. You must be led of the Holy Ghost to do a work of the Lord Jesus Christ. He commanded us to seek the Kingdom of God and all of his righteousness. However, most of what we see being built today is people building their own kingdom. It will not stand in the end. The Spirit of God gives the vision. The Spirit of God gives the instructions and by His Spirit are the works of faith accomplished. The Word tells us that a greater work will we do. Signs, miracles, and wonders will follow the believer.

Isaiah 5:20-21

Woe unto them that call evil good, and good evil; that put darkness for light, and light for darkness: that put bitter for sweet, and sweet for bitter! Woe unto them that are wise in their own eyes, and prudent in their own sight!

2 Kings 5:1-3 & 10-13

Now Naaman, a captain of the host of the king of Syria, was a great me with his master, and honourable because by him the Lord had given deliverance unto Syria: he was also a mighty man in valour, but he was a leper. And the Syrians had gone out by companies and had brought away captive out of the land of Israel a little maid, and she waited on Naaman's wife. And she said unto her mistress would God my Lord were with the prophet that is in Samaria! For he would recover him of his leprosy.

And Elisha sent a messenger unto him, saying, go and wash in Jordon seven times, and thy flesh shall come again to thee and thou shall be clean.

It is righteous to have great expectations of the Spirit of God. Naaman almost missed his blessing/miracle because he had a pre-conceived idea about how healing should take place or how deliverance should take place. There are so many revelations that we could share concerning the testimony of Naaman. However, regarding the righteousness of Jesus Christ we must come before his presence with humility believing that through Jesus Christ all things are possible. He doesn't have a respect of persons. Your rank is not what moves him. Your prestige is not what moves him. Your familial status is not what moves him. The amount of battles you've fought and won is not what moves him. But the faith to believe gets his attention every time and is counted to us as righteousness.

It is good to do righteousness. It is good to seek after the Lord for the indwelling of his Holy Spirit. It is good to speak his word in season and out of season. It is good to let your light shine. It is good to contend for the faith of the Most High. Stand tall and do his will and do his purpose. Pick up your weapons of righteousness and fight!

Feet Shod With The Preparation Of The Gospel Of Peace...

For to be carnally minded is death; but to be spiritually minded is life and peace.   Rom 8:6

It's imperative that we take with us the gospel of peace and fight. We must stand firm on the Word of God and a firm foundation of faith. This scripture reassures us that though we're in a spiritual war, we have life and peace through Christ Jesus.

...how beautiful are the feet of them that preach the gospel of peace and bring glad tidings of good things.   Rom 10:15

A major part of our daily battle is to compel men and women to come to Christ. This is a time for kingdom building. This is one of our main missions. Feed the Sheep. Save that which is lost. You cannot do this without preaching the gospel of peace. Everyone by nature wants peace (most of us).

But now in Christ Jesus ye who were sometimes were afar off are made nigh by the blood of Christ.   Ephesians 2:13-14

For He is indeed our peace...

There is a time for war and time for peace. Though we may be at war now, we have peace to look forward to through Christ Jesus.

Let him eschew evil (turn away from) and do good; let him seek peace and ensue it (pursue).   I Peter 3:11

Just as Jesus is our Prince of Peace, He requires us to be peacemakers as well. Oftentimes, I've fellowshipped with some individuals who claimed to be Christians, but in passing they are rude, crude, and socially undesirable. We have to let our light shine at all times. Sometimes we create our own battles and our own drama because of our negative attitudes. We must operate in the fruits of the Spirit. I know that as you read through this, you may start to get overwhelmed. Don't overthink this, especially those of you who are analytic minded (like myself). God is a simple God; we make things more complex than they have to be. However, to whom much is given, much is also required. The Lord tell us in Psalms 121:1-2, "I will lift up mine eyes unto the hills, from whence cometh my help. My help cometh from the Lord, which made the heaven and earth." Keep in mind that we are not on the battlefield alone. We are helpers of one another, and also, the Lord is always a present help in the time of trouble.

Matthew 10:13-15

And if the house be worthy, let your peace come upon it: but if it be not worthy, let your peace return to you.

And whosoever shall not receive you, nor hear your words, when ye depart out of that house or city, shake off the dust of your feet.

Verily I say unto you, it shall be more tolerable for the land of Sodom and Gomorrah in the day of judgement, than for that city.

When you go forth in the name of the Lord Jesus, no matter how much you come prepared with the Gospel of Peace, many are for war as King David mentioned in a Psalm. The world cannot receive you. So, be not weary in your efforts to bring it forth. The Lord said, if it be possible be peaceable among all men. In some instances, it is not possible because there is no peace without the Prince of Peace. You cannot attempt to unify in the flesh. The unity must first take place in the Holy Spirit. When you're coming to the presence of a group of non-believers whose hearts are not prepared to be converted and healed, then you must shake the dust off your feet. The gifts will make room for the Spirit to move and have His way, even the gift of love. If there is room there, then He will operate because He is a gentleman. Be reminded that the Children of God hear his words and will receive the love in peace. So, put on the whole armor and contend for the faith!

Above All, Taking The Shield Of Faith, Wherewith Ye Shall Be Able To Quench All The Fiery Darts Of The Wicked...

But without faith it is impossible to please Him: for he that cometh to God must believe that He is, and that He is a rewarder of those that diligently seek Him.
Hebrews 11:6

Faith moves God, and there is absolutely no way you can fight in the Lord's army if you don't believe. For this reason, the Lord demands that you make a decision. In Joshua 24:15, He states "…choose ye this day whom you will serve." You have to know that He is God. He is the Alpha and the Omega, the first and the last, the beginning and the end. We must know that He is a God that is able to do all things except fail. Be reminded that faith is the substance of things hoped for, the evidence of things unseen (Hebrews 11:1). We must believe in those things we cannot see. Oftentimes, many of us confess with our mouths state that we believe in the unseen, but we really depend on man because of the things that are tangible, things which we can see. Oftentimes, we refuse to step out on true faith and believe in the unseen. Yet, we are fighting a war against the unseen. We believe in a God that we cannot see. Therefore, we must see the unseen, hear the unseen, feel the unseen, know the unseen. For we have already obtained the evidence of these things we cannot see.

Everything revolves around your faith. Most of us say we have faith right up until we have to put our money to where our mouth is. When we have to walk in it, we often sing another tune. Faith is an action word, just as love is. It requires work, lots of it.

Early in my faith walk, I had several misunderstandings regarding faith. I would go forth, laying hands on the sick, believing for their recovery, and in more than one case, those individuals did not recover. This happened more often than I wanted. Laying hands on the sick wasn't something that I woke up one morning and decided to do; I was given explicit instructions by the Lord to go forth and heal the sick and all manner of illness. So, I went to the hospitals to do this. I was acting out of obedience, so, when the patients weren't healed, I became angry with the Lord. I knew I had the faith and the power, so in my eyes, the Lord wasn't following through on His Word, and after a period of not getting results that I wanted, doubt began to manifest.

We can't stop believing simply because we don't see results right away. God is still God whether he heals, delivers, or sets anyone free at all. He is still the Great I Am. If He doesn't work another miracle ever, He is still God. We cannot believe based on what our eyes see. Our faith cannot fluctuate with our circumstances either. A prime example of this is proclaimed by the three Hebrew boys, who stated in Daniel 3:17-18, "If it be so, our God whom we serve is able to deliver us from the fiery furnace, and He will deliver us out of thine hand, O king. But if not, be it known unto thee that we will not serve thy gods, nor worship the golden image which thou hast set up." The key phrase is, "But if not." regardless, our belief cannot change. The enemy would love for us to stop believing in God. When we doubt God, we don't just doubt His being, we doubt His power and ability to make things happen on our behalf as well as the behalf of others. If our enemy can come as a wile, which will make us doubt the power we have, then in turn we don't use our God-given power, less healing takes place, less deliverance takes place, and overall, we have relinquished our power and authority to our enemy. Once this happens, we may as well say that we have thrown in the towel. Our enemy has done his job. So, more than ever we must operate in extraordinary faith, daring to believe and operate on levels of faith that few have boldly excelled to.

We must look to Jesus who is the author and finisher of our faith...
Hebrews 12:2 (paraphrased)

As we walk daily by faith, we bear the testimony of the Lord Jesus Christ in our lives. There is a reason why we believe. Besides the testimony of our fathers, Jesus designed our testimony of faith to be personal. There is something that persuaded us to believe on the name Jesus Christ. We are troubled on every side, yet not distressed; we are perplexed, but not in despair; persecuted, but not forsaken; cast down, but not destroyed; always bearing about in the body the dying of the Lord Jesus, that the life also of Jesus might be made manifest in our body(2Cor4:10).

Troubles, tests, perplexities and the like are allowed for the glory of God to be manifest in our lives. They make room for trust. By working miracles, signs, and wonders, He establishes the faith in us necessary to contend and overcome. Remember, we are not just fighting on our own behalf, but for the faith of others just a well.

What did Jesus do to win your heart? For Paul it was an encounter on Damascus Road where the Lord approached and addressed his sin and transgressions of persecuting the Children of God. When the revelation of Jesus Christ was shown to him the Lord removed the scales of blinders from his eyes as well as his heart. What about you? The initial testimony that got you to choose Jesus as your personal Lord and Savior that is the core of the shield of faith. That spiritual shield is built of testimony after testimony of the overcoming power of the Most High. With that shield you overcome the wiles of the enemy knowing that if he covered you before, He will do it again. He healed you before, he will heal you again. He delivered you before, he will deliver you again. Through it all, you're carrying the death and resurrection of Christ within you. No matter the circumstance. No matter the situation. The relationship is personal. So, hold that shield high for when the enemy comes like a flood. The Lord Jesus lifts up a standard.

Rom 8:37-39

Nay, in all these things we ae more than conquerors through him that loved us. For I am persuaded, that neither death, nor life, nor angels, nor principalities, nor powers, nor things present, nor things to come, nor height, nor depth, nor any other creature, shall be able to separate us from the Love of God, which is in Christ Jesus our Lord.

      I personally had attended many church services and accepted Jesus Christ as my Savior at a young age. However, the encounter where I was fully persuaded without doubt was when I cried to the Lord with my whole heart. I wanted more from life. I wanted to be loved. I longed for fulfilment in a place deep within my heart that was reserved just for Christ. I was a young adult with many failed relationships. I didn't have a relationship with my parents. My friends were really acquaintances. I lacked self-esteem, self-confidence and it seemed as if I lived my life to please others. I thought they were never satisfied. I had nothing to lose and I cried unto the Lord. He heard my cry. He answered me. He told me He loved me and that nothing was wrong with me. He addressed my spiritual situation and said that he was always there! Before I was formed in the womb, He loved me and had a plan for my life. I laid aside every weight and sin that beset me and I gave it to Jesus Christ who was the author and finisher of my faith. He told me I must live for Him. He chose me and his approval was the only one I needed. That night he confirmed His words of comfort with a sign/miracle. He mended my broken heart. He replaced the hurt and emptiness with love and joy and laughter, and His peace that passed all understanding. The Lord Jesus Christ encountered me with the truth about who I was and what I had done and the truth about who he was and his plan for my life. The truth is what set me free. The truth is my testimony and the truth is what fully persuaded me. The truth is that shield of faith that says to the enemy, we believe the report of the Lord. So, pick up your weapons and fight the good fight of faith!

The Helmet of Salvation

And He saw that there was no man, and wondered that there was no intercessor: therefore, His arm brought salvation unto Him; and His righteousness it sustained Him.

For He put on righteousness as a breastplate, and a helmet of salvation upon his head; and he put on the garments of vengeance for clothing and was clad with zeal a cloke.   Isaiah 59:16-17

      This is one of the reasons why the Lord says put on your whole armor. You absolutely cannot function properly with missing pieces, just as your pants don't fit properly without a belt. Don't get caught with pieces missing from your uniform; it could be costly and could have consequences given accordingly. Besides, I know you wouldn't want one of your fellow soldiers at battle with you to get hurt also because of something you failed to do. I remember my days in basic training with the US Military when my flight had to do flutter kicks because of a mistake I made. I must say that wasn't a good start to the day for me. I was walking around half the day with people who were supposed to be on my side, yet they were upset with me. Anyhow, we must know that we are fighting based on the firm belief that God humbly manifested himself in the flesh (Christ Jesus), walked the earth, was wounded for our transgressions though He was blameless, and came with the sole purpose of dying for our sins that through Christ we may have life everlasting.

And thou child shalt be called the prophet of the Highest; for thou shalt go before the face of the Lord to prepare his ways;

To give knowledge of salvation unto his people by the remission of their sins.
Luke 1:76-77

It's ironic the salvation is worn as a helmet on our head. Because as stated above, it requires knowledge in order to receive salvation. This, too, is why the Word says faith comes by hearing and hearing by the Word of God. So, then how do we obtain knowledge? Romans 10:14 asks the questions for us…How shall they believe in Him of whom they have not heard? And how shall they hear without a preacher? Then the Lord tells us what to do in Mark 16:15:

Go ye into all the world and preach the gospel to every creature.

Remember what it means to be saved. Know the benefits and the rewards of salvation. Don't let the enemy penetrate your mind with thoughts of the past, which will have you question your salvation. God's Word is true and shall not return to Him void. Whom the Son has set free is truly free indeed (John 8:36).

And you being in your sin and the circumcision of your flesh, hath he quickened together with Him, having forgiven you all trespasses;

Blotting out the handwriting of ordinances that was against us, which was contrary to us, and took it out of the way, nailing it to the cross.
Colossians 2:13-14

Persuaded In Your Own Mind

Rom 14:1 & 5

Him that is weak in the faith receive ye, but not to doubtful disputations. One man esteemed one day above another: another esteemeth every day alike. Let every man be fully persuaded in his own mind.

We must seek our own salvation with fear and much trembling. We must also have a ready and willing mind to do the will and purpose of Christ. To maintain a position to be victorious in battle, it is important to walk in the spirit and be in unity with the mind of Christ. The mind plays a major role with regards to the actions a person may or may not take. Before a person acts on something it is often the thoughts that bring forth the actions. A great portion of spiritual warfare is psychological in nature. So, we must be persuaded in our mind that we are a Royal Priesthood, a peculiar people, chosen for sanctification and redeemed by the blood of Jesus Christ. That belief is a helmet. His spirit is a covering from the attacks of the enemy.

2 Cor 10:4

For the weapons of our warfare are not carnal, but mighty through God to the pulling down of strong holds. Casting down imaginations, and every high thing that exalteth itself against the knowledge of God and bringing into captivity every thought to the obedience of Christ.

The enemy will bring imaginations that are high, and they come against the knowledge of the Lord God and His truth. That is a type of psychological warfare waring against the mind of Christ. However, the Lord makes known that our weapons which we utilize to fight such battles are not carnal but are spiritual and mighty through God. We must endure the battlefield of the mind by believing only and standing firm on the promises of God. Speak the Word out of your mouth in season and out. Speak to the situation. Speak those things that be not as though they were.

There will be times when you will hear things in the mind that are contrary to the word. There will also be times where you may dream a dream, or see a vision that is not true or not sent from the Lord. No matter what tactics the enemy attempts to use, kill it on contact! Cast down the vain imaginations, and do not allow them to penetrate the heart and provoke you to actions of doubt and unbelief. Guard your mind with the helmet of salvation. Put on the whole armor. Be watchful and pray. Having done all to stand, stand and see the salvation of the Lord.

Philippians 4:8

Finally, brethren, whatsoever things are true, whatsoever things are honest, whatsoever things are just, whatsoever things are of good report, if there be any virtue, and if there be any praise, think on these things.

So, then faith cometh by hearing and hearing by the Word of God (Romans 10:17). So, pick up your weapons and fight! You are indeed needed on the battlefield!

The Sword Of The Spirit, Which Is The Word Of God

Take a look at all the attire we have so far. You have a girdle, a breastplate, a shield, and a helmet, all of which would be generally recognize as weapons of defense. However, wouldn't you agree that our main offensive weapon would be our sword? Did anyone else get that? There's always an offense and defense. Our Sword is most definitely a powerful weapon! I believe that is why before even obtaining salvation from the Lord, He states that we must first confess with our mouths, then believe in our hearts that He indeed died for our sins and rose on the third day. We must confess the Word of God.

Death and Life are in the power of the tongue: and they that love it shall eat the fruit thereof. *Proverbs 18:21*

Throughout our daily spiritual battle, we must learn to use the Word of God against our enemies. Be reminded that when Jesus fasted and went into the wilderness to be tempted by Satan for forty days and forty nights, He always rebutted the enemy's nonsense with the Word of God. We have the power and authority to say to any mountain or any problem to be cast into the sea, and it shall be done.

And God said Let us make man in our own image, after our likeness and let them dominion over the fish of the sea, and over the foul of the air, and over the cattle, and over all the earth, and over every creeping thing that creepeth upon the earth.

Genesis 1:26

We must shove the Word of God right down the enemy's throat! Remember, everything is spiritual. However, the Lord given to us the authority to rebuke the enemy in the name of Jesus! We must always utilize the spiritual authority given to us through Christ. We cannot expect Him to do the impossible If we don't first do what's possible. This where the works come in. He tells us that faith without works is dead. We must first use what he has given us and work with it. In in the beginning, God created the heavens and the earth by speaking the words out of His mouth. Then He said, "let there be light," and there was light. And God said, "Let the earth bring forth grass."

The Lord spoke saying: for as the rain cometh down, and the snow from heaven, and return not tither, but watereth the earth, and maketh it bring forth and bud, that it may give seed to the sower, and bread to the eater:

So, shall my word be that goeth forth out of my mouth: it shall not return unto me void, but it shall proper in the thing whereto I sent it.
Isaiah 55:10-11

I'm a firm believer that the very same goes to us because we were created in the same image and have been given the same authority through Christ Jesus. Whatever we speak out our mouths shall bring forth fruit, whether it be positive or negative. James 3:8-10 gives more insight:

For the tongue can no man tame: it is an unruly evil, full of deadly poison. Therewith bless we God, even the father; and therewith curse we men, which is made after the similitude of God.
Out of the same mouth proceedeth blessing and cursing...

Isn't it absolutely amazing that the scripture mentions the tongue as being deadly poison? Why not then use our deadly poison against our enemies instead of against our fellow soldiers in Christ? Our fighting is in vain if we are using our weapons against each other. We wind up making the devil's job a whole lot easier, wouldn't you agree? So, we must be careful with what we say of our mouths. We can bring curses against ourselves with our very own weaponry. For this reason, we should follow behind David, for he proclaims in Psalms 34:1," I will bless the Lord at all times: His praise shall continually be in my mouth." We must eat, live, and breathe the Word. We must meditate on it both day and night. The Word is what sustains us and what will keep us. All things shall fall, but the Word of God shall stand. Another thing I must mention is that oftentimes we focus on hiding the Word in our hearts, but we must also be sure that it reigns supreme in our minds as well.

Personally, I've always been analytically minded, a "thinker", some would call it. It's a trait that's been ingrained in my personality. At times when I had my guard down, the devil had a field day with my mind. To one who is an analyst, this could be your downfall if you're not careful. You may be asking,"How does this correlate with the Word of God?" The truth is that the Word has to saturate your mind. Just take a minute and picture a coffee pot. Now imagine thoughts in your mind being the coffee granules in the filter. Once the water is poured in, the coffee is brewed and flows down into the carafe. Imagine the carafe being your heart. The point is that every action you choose to go forth in often originates first in the mind. So, if the Word penetrates the mind and flows to the heart, then the actions that spring forth will be of holiness and righteousness, you're reaping victory in every dimension. Aren't you excited?

How can you be the most effective and victorious in battle? You must be in complete unity with the Lord Jesus Christ. You must know him. To know him you must be one with the word. He is the word. He said, in the beginning was the Word. The Word was with God. And the Word is God.

2 Timothy 2:15

Study to shew thyself approved unto God, a workman that needeth not to be ashamed, rightly dividing the Word of Truth.

The Lord urges us as servants to seek him through his word. Get to know him. Receive his Holy Spirit to withstand in the evil day. This is a sense of urgency to learn what the will of the Lord is in your life. Learn his precepts. Seek after His Spirit to learn the operations of His Spirit while He is yet willing. This way you learn what the difference between his voice and you own voice and even understand when they're one. As you continue to hide the Word of God even to increase your own faith and belief. Faith comes by hearing so, by continuing to speak the word we continue to build and activate our most Holy Faith.

2 Cor 4:13

We having the same spirit of faith, according as it is written, I believed and therefore have I spoken; we also believe and therefore speak; knowing that we which raised up the Lord Jesus shall raise us up also by Jesus Christ, and shall present us with you.

The word must come forth. It cannot return void, but most perform the will of the Lord. What we cannot do is allow the enemy to silence us. Our enemies must comply to the commands of the Word of God. Keep speaking the word. Write the word. Sing the word. Pray the word. It shall come to pass. When it is mingled with faith the enemies tremble.

Heb 4:12

For the word of God is quick, and powerful, and sharper than any two-edged sword, piercing even to the dividing asunder of soul and spirit, and of the joints and marrow, and is a discerner of the thoughts and the intents of the heart.

Jesus Christ is the bread of life with emphasis on the word "life". The word is our lively hope. He quickens and brings forth life. The word is also so powerful and sharp that when used it can even divide a soul and spirit. What the scripture is sharing is judgement with the Word of God. This is the demonstration of the Power of God by his Holy Word. While demonic forces are ever present warring for our very soul, the word divides the spirit from the soul. This is deliverance. He sets captives free by his word.

Praying Always With All Supplication…

Why not pray to the head general from whom your orders originated to begin with? Communication is crucial in war. It is through communication that we are able to get understanding of our missions and get updates on the effectiveness of your penetrations against our enemy's strongholds. The Lord says in 1Thessalonians 5:17 to Pray without ceasing.

Watch therefore and pray always that ye may be accounted worthy to escape all these things that shall come to pass, and to stand before the son of man.

We must pray so that we can communicate our status and advise our position on the battlefield because angels are sent to fight on our behalf as well. Take note in Daniel 10:12-13 when the archangel Michael was sent to assist Daniel after many days of prayers:

Then said he unto me, fear not Daniel for from the first day that thou didst set thine heart to understand and to chasten thyself before thy God, thy words were heard, and I am come for thy words.

But the prince of the kingdom of Persia withstood me one and twenty days: but, lo Michael, one of the chief princes, came to help me; and I remained there with the kings of Persia.

So, here we see clearly that it was because of Daniel's fervent prayers and supplications that the Lord did indeed send assistance to Daniel in his time of need. Prayer is definitely a necessity so that you can have effectiveness against spiritual wickedness on earth, as well as the heavenlies. This all goes hand and hand with seeking God's face while He yet may be found. We cannot seek His face without prayer. The Lord said that those who seek Him early shall surely find Him. Have you ever heard the saying, "the early bird gets the worm?" Well, I've found that saying to be true. If you want God to show favor, try seeking Him in the wee hours of the morning, or as a mother would call it zero dark thirty, and see if you don't find Him. The Lord will recognize the sacrifice of your time, but most will agree with me to say they would be sacrificing sleep as well.

The Bible says that at midnight, Paul and Silas prayed and sang praises to God while they were in prison. Then the Lord intervened on their behalf and broke them out of the prison. See, the battle really isn't even ours, it's the Lord's. How great thou art! It's an absolute honor to be chosen as a warrior for the Lord because when you come and think of it, He really doesn't need us to do anything for Him. He's given us the privilege. Remember, He is the creator or all things! If the scripture says acknowledge the Lord in all our ways and He will direct our paths, then how is this possible if we don't pray? We're fighting a losing battle if we don't listen for God to order every one of our steps. Please notice that I mentioned that prayer is a communication and that communication is a three-way process. You're communicating with God and God communicates with you, but also Romans 8:26-27 confirms that "Likewise the Spirit also helpeth our infirmities: for we know not what we should pray as we ought: but the Spirit itself maketh intercession for us with groanings which cannot be uttered. And he that searcheth the hearts, knoweth what is the mind of the Spirit, because He maketh intercession for the saints according to the will of God."

So, some of the things that we don't even know to pray for, the Holy Spirit intervenes and prays for on our behalf. I also believe that it goes vice versa as well, because many of us pray prayers but don't bother to sit for a minute to listen for a possible response. The Lord doesn't always make us wait for an answer, so there are times when the Holy Spirit holds the information within our Spirit until we ae in a position to receive it.

There was a period of time in my life when everything that could be shaken was shaken. There were days when I couldn't pray anymore in English. I had to pray in the Spirit. I had to let the Spirit utter things, which I couldn't imagine speaking. Being the analytic-minded person that I am, I tried everything that my little mind could think to do, I prayed all the prayers I could think to pray, but sometimes you have to let go, pray in the Spirit, then shut up… and listen.

It's important to read all the scripture in its fullness which finishes by stating that we be "in the Spirit." For Jesus is a Spirit and therefore must be worshipped in Spirit and in truth. Well, we've heard it from the Apostle Paul as well that we must die daily, meaning that we must die to the flesh so that we may operate in the Spirit. Praying in the Sprit is our weapon of warfare. This is our communication with the Father that the enemy cannot understand and therefore cannot penetrate. There is a military type alphabet, which allows you to communicate things in forms that the enemy cannot understand. You may recall something like "alpha, bravo, Charlie…" Well, our prayer language where we pray in the Spirit is similar. The enemy cannot penetrate that line of communication. He cannot stop that prayer in its track because has he no clue what we're saying.

There may have been occasions where you may have felt weak and spiritually drained. One of the ways to rebuild your spiritual strength is to utilize your prayer language, which may also be known to many as speaking in tongues. This is for your edification. This is a part of protecting your anointing. When you're doing work for the Lord, for example, you may be one who will lay hands on the sick that they may recover. Well, virtue leaves your body, and one of the ways to restore strength is to pray in the spirit. This is a major part of seeking the face of God because it must be done in the spirit. Make sure that one of the first things you do when going into prayer is to sincerely repent of your sins; especially those who have the indwelling of the Holy Ghost. We don't want to come before God unclean. We want to be sure our prayers are heard and responded to. The Word of God states that the effectual, fervent prayers of the righteous availeth much.

If you pray to God without repentance and without cleansing yourself of the spirits you've been subject to throughout the day, then you risk praying prayers that are outside the will of God. For example, if all week long you've been entertaining a hate spirit and have not cleansed yourself, though you may not have a physically done anything wrong, that spirit takes the forefront, and in the spirit realm that spirit is what is praying. Of course, that spirit will pray prayers of demise and harm. This is a form of witchcraft, and in most cases, you can do it and not even realize it. These prayers aren't answered by God. I will discuss more of this subject in later chapters.

When we walk our daily walk in the Lord as time goes by it is rather easy to get complacent and settled in the confidence of the salvation. However, the Lord urges and encourages us to take heed those who think they are standing. The enemy will not come through the front or back door. Therefore, we pray so that we may abide in the vine. The Lord warns us that the temptations we encounter throughout our day to day seek are those that are simple and common to man. Meaning that there is nothing new under the sun. Most of what is being done in this earth has already been done. Therefore, we must pray to be kept by him because He is our way of escape in times of trouble.

Overcoming Selfish Praying Habits

1 Cor 10:33

Even as I please all men in all things, not seeking mine own profit, but the profit of many, that they may be saved.

When we pray, we should make sure the Lord's will is manifested. As the word states, we may want to please our brethren, however, we must pray for edification. We must pray that the needs are met so that many will be saved. Some need signs, miracles, and wonders. Some need food and shelter. Some need the Word of God. Yet, in all things we desire the perfection of the Body of Christ, whatever the need may be. When we pray, we must be selfless. We are not seeking for our own, but for the profit of others. You are a servant, so serve with humility and much prayer and supplication on behalf of the saints of the Most High. We ought to seek that we are in position to perfect that which may be lacking in the faith.

James 1:6-7

But let him ask in the faith, nothing wavering. For he that wavereth is like a wave of the sea driven with the wind and tossed. For let not that man think that he shall receive anything of the Lord.

We must believe when we pray. We know that without faith it is impossible to please the Lord and that when we pray by his spirit believing only it is then that he will hear us from heaven and give us the desires of our heart. We must not pray amiss. This means that we must not pray simply to fulfil the lusts of the flesh. When we approach the lord, the word also allows for us to discern the righteous path of God. He allows us by his word to search the deep things of God even the intents of the heart. The discernment gives us the ability to know who has our best interest at heart and the true intentions of others we encounter by the Spirit. When utilized properly, the discernment will have you to gain the advantage on the battlefield for Christ. Be sure to apply the word to your life and contend for the faith.

Praying By The Spirit

Psalms 24:3

He that hath clean hands, and a pure heart, who hath not lifted up his soul unto vanity, nor sworn deceitfully.

Purity is a virtue. The things that we do in Christ must be with purity and integrity. We must remember that Jesus purchased us with his blood. We do not work on our own accord but according to the will and purpose of Christ. Therefore, when we communicate, we speak with desire to have necessity to accomplish and fulfil our mission in Christ. Being that we belong to God, we take orders from Him. We are not doing our own will and because of this, effective communication with the Lord is most necessary. We need constant instruction and intel to maintain righteousness in the earth and to be sure we ourselves do not go astray. We must decrease and He must increase within us. To do so requires surrender and prayer.

1 Cor 10:12-13

Wherefore let him that thinketh he standeth take heed lest he fall.

There hath no temptation taken you but such as is common to man: but God is faithful, who will not suffer you to be tempted above that ye are able; but will with the temptation also make a way of escape, that ye may be able to bear it.

While the prayers that we pray should be pure, we should pray that we are able to stand and overcome temptation. When we pray in the spirit, we are praying for ourselves as well as other members of the Body of Christ. Through prayer we build each other and tear the Kingdom of Satan down.

We are to approach the Lord in sincerity of heart. There are some who pray for things so that they may consume it with their own lusts and to indulge in covetous practices. This ought not be done. So, we ought not ask for a new expensive vehicle to show it off to the neighbor who also recently purchased one. You should not petition the Lord for another man's husband or wife because you feel that it is better for them to be with you than in their current situation. When a desire is an unrighteous desire it is considered a covetous practice. However, Jesus is the God of Grace and Mercy. We can pray for the Lord's deliverance from such desires that are not pleasing in his sight. He said that we may come boldly come to the throne of grace. That's what makes a prayer pure, when you approach him in truth laying aside every weight and sin that does so easily beset us. We place it all at the feet of Jesus. His yoke is easy. His burden is light.

How many times have you seen someone in an unhealthy relationship? Maybe there was domestic abuse. Maybe there was infidelity. We cannot add sin to sin with the hopes that grace may abound. We pray for complete deliverance. We pray for healing. We pray for hearts to be mended and that those who are captives be set free in the name of Jesus. We pray seeking to discern what the will of the Lord is.

Matthew 6:7-13

But when ye pray, use not vain repetitions, as the heathen do: for they think that they shall be heard for their much speaking. Be not ye therefore like unto them: for your father knoweth what things ye have need of before ye ask of him. After this manner therefore pray ye: our Father which art in Heaven, hallowed be thy name. Thy kingdom come. Thy will be done in earth, as it is in Heaven.

Give us this day our daily bread. And forgive us our debts, as we forgive our debtors. And lead us not into temptation but deliver us from evil: for thine is the kingdom, and the power, and the glory, forever. Amen.

The Lord has given us instructions on the way to pray in a way that would please the Father. The word tells us that we must first believe that he is and that he is a rewarder of them that diligently seek after the Lord. We give honor and acknowledge that the Lord abides in Heaven. We hallow his name as to say that he is God alone. He is sanctified. He is set aside. He is the all-seeing, all knowing, and the only wise God.

While praying to the Lord we should pray with expectation of living with him on high, yet by faith and belief through prayer we are entering the kingdom with our petition. With our words of supplication, we also have a mission to maintain that the Lord's perfect will which is manifest in the heavens and is also manifested in the earth. Then, He says, "Give us this day our daily bread." Meaning that the Lord stated that He came that we may have life and we would have it more abundantly. However, what we ask of Him is our daily necessities to sustain us so that we can accomplish the will and purpose of Christ. Then, the Lord states in the prayer that we repent of our sins but suggests that our repentance will be received with the condition that we forgive others that may have wronged us. Lead us not into temptation. We know that the Lord is a good shepherd. He will never lead us in the wrong direction. He will not tempt us but desires our trust in times of temptation. He will deliver us for his glory. In Jesus is the kingdom, and power, and glory. In this we acknowledge Jesus has created all things for himself and he is the author of all glory, honor, and power. While praying we approach the throne of grace believing only knowing that God is not a man that he should lie or the Son of Man that he should repent. When we pray according to his will, and he will perform it.

Earlier in my walk with Christ I did a lot of praying for myself and crying out to the Lord. Most of my prayers were selfish, however, it was necessary to grow in the faith. It is better to communicate with the Lord about all things than to lean to your own understanding. The more you communicate with the Lord Jesus and give it all to him, you're decreasing so that the Spirit of God may increase. That way you are not quenching the Spirit or grieving the Spirit. Though initially your prayers are somewhat selfish, it's edifying when you stay on the potter's wheel. Much of your prayer life in the beginning is getting to know the voice of God and deciphering his voice from your own. While also knowing when the two are one. He wants us to know him and to know our role in him. You must know who you are in Christ. These things require much prayer to understand the will of the Lord. When the Lord works on you and shapes you, then you have removed the beam out of thine own eye so that you can effectively assist a brother or sister remove the mote from theirs.

An unhealthy selfishness is when you have repetitive prayers or prayers of anxiety as if the Lord doesn't know your situation or circumstance. He knows what we are going through and has already made a way by his Spirit even before situations occur. There is no sense in being anxious for anything. We walk by faith, not by sight. We must trust and wait on the Lord. We cannot control anything. We cannot manipulate anything to move in one direction or another. Faith, obedience, and praise move God. You cannot control time or sensitive issues that are designed for the Lord's glory. You must maintain your integrity and your sincerity. You put things in the Lord's hands and leave it there. Do not pick it up again.

There was a time when I was working with a very tight income. With the budget I had no room for error. There came a point when I didn't know where the rent would come from or how. I prayed with faith and then I praised all night long. I didn't have any other options. I had nothing to lose. The Lord showed favor and provided for all my needs according to his riches in glory.

In the days of my youth, I wasn't faithful. I would have floated a check and prayed to God that the money was there before it bounced. However, the Lord does things in decency and in order. He doesn't want you running like a jack rabbit bouncing from here to there asking as if your Father in Heaven hasn't heard you. He wants you to be unshakeable, unmovable, and ever abounding from faith to faith and glory to glory. So, stand tall knowing that your Father can do all things but fail.

PUTTING ON OUR GARMENT OF PRAISE

Praise is an extremely important part of our spiritual weaponry, believe it or not. Though it may not be mentioned along with our other weapons in Ephesians, it is indeed a powerful offensive, as well as defensive weapon. My husband, a prophet, has oftentimes said to me, "Don't wait until the battle is over; shout now." See, when you've presented yourself to God as a living sacrifice, holy and acceptable, you've taken up your cross and stated, "For Jesus I live and for Jesus I die.", you move up on the enemy's list of priorities. However, praise is what gets you through it all. The enemy and all of his demons hate to hear the praises of God's people. Praise breaks yolks and the strongholds of our enemy.

To appoint unto them that mourn in Zion, to give unto them beauty for ashes, the oil of joy for mourning, the garment of praise for the spirit of heaviness; that they might be called the trees of righteousness, the planting of the Lord, that He might be glorified.

Isaiah 61:13

The Lord assures us in the scripture that praise is a cure for a spirit of heaviness. You see that praise not only fights off the enemy, but it all around makes us feel better, for the Lord inhabits the praises of His people. Praise goes hand in hand with faith, and faith moves God.

When I first accepted my calling, recognizing that I was indeed a chosen vessel of the Most High, I began to be tried by fire, and that fire is hot! However, praising God through it all just for who He is, is more powerful than we can begin to imagine. Remember the scripture in Acts from the previous chapter where I mentioned Paul and Silas? Well, the same goes for praise as well. When Paul and Silas sang praises unto God, it moved God to break them out of prison.

During the reign of Hezekiah, Isaiah came forth with a word from the Lord, informing Hezekiah that he was soon to die. Hezekiah began to plead his case to the Lord, bringing all of the good deeds to memory that he had done. However, it wasn't until he stated that "the grave cannot praise you," that he was given a fifteen-year extension on his life. There is power in praise!

For the grave cannot praise thee, death cannot celebrate thee: they that go down into the pit cannot hope for thy truth. The living, the living, he shall

praise thee, as I do this day: the father to the children shall make know thy truth.
Isaiah 38:18-19

Praise brings us closer to God.

Draw nigh to God, and He will draw night to you. Cleanse your hands, ye sinners; purity your hearts ye double minded.

James 4:8

In order to break down flesh, get into the spiritual realm of things, and get into a better position to hear from God, praise is required.

For they that are after the flesh do mind the things of the flesh; but they that are after the Spirit, the things of the Spirit.

For to be carnally minded is death; but to be spiritually minded is life and peace.

So, they that are in the flesh cannot please God.

Romans 8:5-6,8

With that being said, we can also conclude that we cannot please God without praise, because praise breaks down flesh. I believe this is also why we can praise God for hours in "fleshly time", but in the spiritual realm, it seems as if hardly any time has passed at all! There is no concept of time in the spiritual realm.

Some time ago, the Lord shared a mystery with me regarding praise and my enemies. The Lord said that my praise would reveal to me who my enemies are and what their secret plots and strategies are. There were times when I became so angry at things my enemies were doing that I would sit and cry out to God for hours. Then the Lord began to minister to me that He required more of me than just prayer and that I also need to rise to another level in praise. To expedite the process of my enemies being handled, I had to praise God on new levels. Every time I thought of my enemies and their plots, I praised God like had never praised before. No matter the time, all through the week. I'd give an offensive praise to handle my enemies before they made another move. I'd give a defensive praise for what they had already done. Every time the devil would send familiar spirits to torment me with things my enemies thought they had gotten away with; I began to praise God. I must admit this was a true breakthrough of my spiritual growth, which had me catapult to new heights in Christ. I went to new dimensions that were unexplainable. My personal relationship with Christ changed forever. Once you get wrapped up and tied up in praise, the things that you once thought bothered you won't seem to matter anymore. That's why I love the psalm of David 27:4, which states: "One thing have I desired of the Lord, that will I seek after; that I may dwell in the house of the Lord all the days of my life, to behold the beauty of the Lord, and to inquire in his temple."

Praise also brings out our spiritual gifts, which are considered spiritual weaponry as well. As a child of God, many of us are born with spiritual gifts to be used for the uplifting of the Kingdom of God. Some of these gifts may include singing, song writing, wisdom, knowledge, and the list goes on. Though I was pre-destined to be a pastor, the only gift I can recall as a child is wisdom. For some reason, I could do anything. I could put anything together, and I could learn any subject without struggle. I even found myself knowing the answers to questions that I had no prior knowledge of. However, other spiritual gifts didn't come until years later through my praise. As I praised God, my singing got better, I grew more knowledgeable of spiritual things, and I also received spiritual understanding. Things became clearer with my praise.

After years of pastoring and increased praise, my prophetic gift manifested, and the Lord began to communicate with me directly the things of the past, present, and the things to come. Because of my praise, my anointing increased, and I obtained more power to preach, heal, and change lives through signs and wonders. God truly inhabits the praised of His people, and where the Spirit of the Lord is, there is liberty (2 Corinthians 3:17).

In preceding chapters, we discussed prayer and how prayers must be pure. Nonetheless, a portion of the process to accomplish purity before the Lord thy God is to praise him with your whole heart. His presence liberates you from the care of this life and from any demonic forces which are attempting to bring you into bondage and weigh you down. Elevate beyond the care, troubles, the situations and circumstances with your praises.

The Lord Jesus encourages us to enter his gates with thanksgiving and enter his courts with praise. The Bible tells us that what's bound on earth is bound in heaven and what's loosed on earth is loosed in heaven. Praise lifts the spirits of heaviness and sets captives free. With your praise you confuse the enemy and you boldly state that God is your keeper and a very present help in the time of trouble. You are stating to the Lord Jesus that you trust him no matter what position you're in, whether you are abased or whether you are abounding. He reigns when you're going through trials and tests.

It's almost as if the enemy is attempting to put blinders on you. Remember, he comes to steal, kill, and destroy. He wants to annihilate you. So, if he can cloud your judgement he will. The enemy wants you to go astray. He wants you to give up and not be able to see the clear path toward the gates of righteousness. However, when you praise the Lord Jesus, his Holy Spirit brings forth remembrance of the testimony he has established within you.

When you praise the Lord, you're renewing your mind to the mind of Christ. You're no longer focused on the problems, circumstances, or frustrations that come with the cares of life, but you're coming into unity with Jesus Christ by his Spirit who has the solution to all of your issues, whatever they may be. Then when you come from praising the Lord, suddenly things come into perspective and the things that you're faced with seem so much smaller than they were before.

Praise Brings Healing

Jesus is a specialist. Healing is His specialty.

The Spirit of the Lord God is upon me; because the Lord hath anointed me to preach good tidings unto the meek; he hath sent me to bind up the broken hearted, to proclaim liberty to the captives and the opening of the prison to them that are bound; to proclaim the acceptable year of the Lord, and the day of vengeance of our God; to comfort all that mourn. Isaiah 61:1-2

God showed us that surgery was possible when he put Adam to sleep and took his rib and formed Eve so that he would not be alone. His work was perfect. There are times when trauma presents situations that require a divine surgical procedure. In Adam's case the issue was loneliness. The Lord knows what we stand in need of even before we ask. He's a mender of broken hearts. When you praise the Lord with your whole heart the Lord starts his procedure of healing every broken place starting with you heart, your mind, and your spirit. Then, when it once seemed like you were a broken cistern that couldn't hold water, as a potter, he molds you. The brokenness is mended. You can hold water again. What he pours into you by his Holy Spirit, it remains. Then you can stir up what's in you and He can use you to pour upon others with your testimony of his righteousness upon your life.

When the Lord approached me and advised me that he had called me and chosen me for a work, I was a mess. Most of my issues that the Lord had to address dealt with the way I perceived myself. I have always loved the Lord, but I didn't like myself. A great bit of spiritual warfare was in the battlefield of the mind. The enemy would often remind me of my short comings and have me to look at all of the wrong in my life. I was shy. I was an outcast. "No one cares. No one is listening to me," I would say to the Lord. "I don't have enough of your spirit," I said. The Lord gently shared with me that I needed to praise him. Lift him up. The more you praise the Lord, the more you will see things clearly. He said everything I needed was in his Spirit. So, praise him for his manifested presence. When I made praise a part of my daily seek, my perspective changed from looking at the wretchedness of the flesh, to accepting the righteousness of Christ. Every wrong was made righteous by his Spirit. No flesh can glory in his presence. The flesh cannot please the Lord. The flesh is wretched, and we are all filthy as rags. Jesus by faith is our righteousness. We must praise the Lord to hear his voice clear on such matters through praise. I can hide myself in Christ. So, that He would be seen and not me. It is then I would be more in sync with doing his will and not my own.

Psalms 100

Make a joyful noise unto the Lord, all ye lands. Serve the Lord with gladness: come before his presence with singing.

Praise is an action of faith toward God. Faith moves God and because of your faith and praise he shows up on your behalf and changes situations. So, activate your most Holy Faith and praise ye the Lord!

FRIENDLY FIRE

In spiritual war (which is every day), we must always be spiritually aware. The enemy's job is to steal, kill, and destroy. With Christians, the enemy knows he can't come in through the front door or through the back door, so he'll attempt to come through the side door. Oftentimes, the side door is friends and family- those in your inner circle. Take time to read over the story of Tamar, David's daughter.

And it came to pass after this, that Absalom, the son of David, had a fair sister, whose name was Tamar; and Amnon, the son of David loved her.

And Amnon was so vexed that he fell sick for his sister Tamar; for she was a virgin; and Amnon thought it hard for him to do anything to her.

But Amnon had a friend whose names was Jonadab, the son of Shimeah, David's brother: and Jonadab was a very subtil man.

And he said unto him, why art thou being the king's son lean from day to day? Wilt thou not tell me? And Amnon said unto him, I love Tamar, my brother Absalom's sister.

And Jonadab said unto him, Lay thee down on thy bed, and maketh thyself sick: and when thy father cometh to see thee, say unto him, I pray thee, let me sister Tamar come, and give me meat, and dress the meat in my sight that I might see it, and eat it at her hand.

So, Amnon lay down, and maketh himself sick: and when the king was come to see him, Amnon said unto the king, I pray thee, let Tamar my sister come, and make me a couple of cakes in my sight, that I may eat at her hand.

Then David sent home to Tamar, saying, go now to thy brother Amnon's house, and dress him meat.

So, Tamar went to her brother Amnon's house; and he was laid down, and she took flour, and kneaded it, and made cakes in his sight, and did bake the cakes.

And she took a pan and poured them out before him; and he refused to eat. And Amnon said, have out all thy men from me. And they went out every man from him. And Amnon said unto Tamar, bring the meat into my chamber, that I may eat of thine hand. And Tamar took the cakes which she made and brought them into the chamber to Amnon her brother. And when she had brought them unto him to eat, he took hold of her, and said unto her, come lie with me sister.

And she answered him, nay, my brother, do not force me; for no such thing ought to be done in Israel: do not thou this folly.

And I, wither shall I cause my shame to go? And as for thee, thou shalt be as one of the fools in Israel. Now therefore, I pray thee, speak unto the king: for he will not withhold me from thee. Howbeit he would not hearken unto her voice: but, being stronger than she, forced her, and lay with her. Then Amnon hated her exceedingly; so that the hatred wherewith he hated her was greater than the love wherewith he loved her. And Amnon said unto her, arise, be gone.

And she said unto him, there is no cause: this evil in sending me away is greater than the other that thou didst unto me. But he would not hearken unto her.

Then he called his servant that ministered unto him, and said, put now this woman out from me, and bolt the door after her.

And she had a garment of divers colours upon her: for with such robes were the king's daughters that were virgins appareled. Then his servant brought her out and bolted the door after her.

And Tamar put ashes on her head and rent her garment of divers colours that was on her, and laid her hand on her head, and went on crying.

Can you see after reading this story how the enemy uses even the ones who are nearest and dearest to us to hurt us? So, in spiritual war, we call this "friendly fire" because these fiery darts that hurt us come from those who are supposed to be on our side in battle. They come at times we least expect it.

Tamar went in to help and assist her brother. She had a heart to love her brother in the way that a sister is supposed to love her brother. She wanted to nurse him back to health. How many of you can say the same about your friends and family? Oftentimes, we may go into a situation with a willingness to serve and assist, and never in our wildest dreams could imagine that our own flesh and blood would even be capable of doing any type of evil, but they do. It happens all the time. However, we mustn't look at face value, because it's the demonic force behind it all.

Oftentimes, we have our guard down to a friend, family member, and all those in our inner circles. We have a certain level of trust, even for those in our circle that claim to be Christians; sometimes they are the main ones. Many of us every day entertain certain spirits, and those of us who don't continue to stay prayed up and spiritual-minded can get caught up with spirits without realizing it. Before long, they begin to have a stronger and stronger hold up us, which makes it harder for us to reach out and get full deliverance from the issue on our own. For example, you can entertain a lying spirit, or lust, anger, or covetous practices.

The story of Tamar and Amnon shows that he was dealing with a lust spirit, spirit of rape, and who knows what else. First, he loved her, then he hated her, and finally he rejected her on top of everything else. Yet, this was a family member. You may think, oh, that was only an isolated case, but let me tell you that things like this happen all the time. Things we have gone through may not have happened to that extreme, but if we can look back on many of the things that the Lord has brought us through, we can concur that many of our painful moments, hurts, or disappointments came from family and friends, husbands and wives. We don't even see it coming most times because within our own hearts we set out to do right, but we can't expect everyone to have a heart like ours all the time. However, we cannot assume, but we must stay prayed up. The Lord will reveal a great bit of things if we would seek Him for the revelation. The Holy Spirit in us is not a respecter of persons.

There is a war going on, and whomever the enemy can use, he will use; no one is exempt.

In Psalm 55:12-13, David cried out the same way many of us have done stating:

It was not my enemy that reproached me: then I could have borne it: neither was it he that hated me that did magnify himself against me; then I would have hid myself from him:

But it was thou, a man of mine equal, my guide, and mine acquaintance.

Here, in this scripture, David confirms the very same thoughts and feelings many of us have experienced. It wasn't our enemy that reproached us because, of course, if we saw our enemy coming, then we could have been prepared. We could have run, we could have hidden ourselves, we could have put our guards up. However, when the blow comes with our guards down, it hurts so much more. That's why the Lord says to trust in no man, but put your trust in Him. This is a war! Sleep with one eye open! Pick up your weapons and fight!

I know many of us can't fathom the idea of friends and family turning on us. It does happen and will happen as long as you're serving God. As Solomon proclaimed, "There is nothing new under the sun" (Ecclesiastes 1:9). Remember the days of old; history repeats itself. Cain killed Abel. Jacob tricked Esau out of selling his birthright and stole his blessing. It was Job's own wife who told him to curse God and die. Even Job's closest friends tried to convince him that he did something wrong and urged him to repent. We must sanctify ourselves and separate ourselves unto holiness and righteousness. Sometimes, this means we must leave family and friends behind. I don't know about you, but I know that I do not want to go to hell for anyone. Jesus already did that.

One of the toughest things I had to learn to do in my walk with Jesus was to yield to discernment and go with what revelation was given based on that discernment. I love the Word of God and love to teach others. Because of the passionate pursuit after God's own heart sometimes I pushed a little past boundaries (ok...maybe a lot beyond boundaries) because of that love. It is one thing to have discernment. It's another to be obedient to His instructions.

Many of my issues regarding friendly fire was my failure to see what was right in front of me. My actions reflected that I wanted my enemies to be my friend. It can be kind of confusing when you think about it. Love can be abounding sometimes especially when it's pure. Love covers a multitude of sins. There were times where the writing was on the wall. The Lord showed me a person's intentions were not good toward me. They did not have my best interest at heart. However, as a pastor I looked at it as a project. I would tell myself they just need some mercy. They need someone to till the ground of their heart. I would see the need for Jesus and run straight toward the fire.

In the meanwhile, discernment said, "maintain a distance." "Give them some seeds and leave it there." You're going to get yourself hurt. Guard your heart." That's what discernment said, often.

After being broken and beaten so many times and crying out to the Lord, He put the pieces of my heart back together. I learned the fear of the Lord and the ability to be humbler than I was. I couldn't do my own will. I was not their savior, Jesus was!

In the process of humility, I learned to decrease, pray, and ask the right questions. I asked, "Do they belong to you, Lord?" What would you have me do in this situation? Is this situation for your glory or for the operations of your spirit? I had to receive the revelation that there are tares planted amongst the wheat. We cannot look on the outward appearance. Jesus searches the reigns of the heart. There are good trees and good fruits as well as there are bad trees not yielding fruit. You cannot change the tree without a miracle.

It really takes surrender and sensitivity to hear what the Holy Spirit is saying and allowing wisdom to apply righteous judgment to a situation. You take yourself down a notch in the purest of love in faith to say that you're here simply as a servant of the Most High and lo, it is written in the volume of the book to do thy will o' Lord. When you condescend to the lowly estate such as that, you eliminate a lot of what seems to be friendly fire because with effective communication with the Lord, He tells you who belongs to Him and who are wolves in sheep's clothing. Just ask and it shall be given. It saves you from a lot of unnecessary wounds.

Know Them That Labor Among You

1 Thess 5:12

And we beseech you, brethren, to know them which labour among you, and are over you in the Lord, and admonish you;

The Lord is pleading with us in this scripture to know the others that are laboring among us in the faith. Know the members of the body so that the Body of Christ is balanced. We stir up the gifts and perfect that which may be lacking with each other, seeking first the Kingdom of God as commanded by God. The more we know them that are laboring with us, the easier it becomes to see the difference when there is someone not belonging to the body and therefore being able to avoid friendly fire, when possible. When you're in sync with the Lord's Spirit, you walk like him, and talk like him, and act like him. As the word says, we know them by their fruits.

The Right Place At The Right Time

Sometimes friendly fire occurs because some of us are not in the right place at the right time. When Jesus Christ gives an instruction, be obedient. Blessings take place simply because you're in the right place abiding in the will and purpose of Christ. Likewise, devastation could happen when you're not in your respective place in Christ. It's also not by chance that you're doing the Lord's will and while you're going along you meet someone who has a phone number you need or a resource to get you to your next step in the faith walk. All things work together for the good of them who are called according to his will and purpose. We walk by faith and not by sight. Sometimes you don't know why you're doing things; you just know you were given instructions. There is a time to trust the Lord and know that you're in his hands and he's working things on your behalf.

Intent Changes With Knowledge

See Isaiah 39

There was an account with Hezekiah after he recovered from his sickness. He was visited by messengers from Babylon with letters and gifts from their king. Hezekiah was so excited having been recovered that he showed the men all that the Lord had done and how he had blessed him so. He held nothing back. This circumstance prompted the Lord to send the Prophet Isaiah with a message concerning what he had done. He prophesied that they would soon return to take it all!

The Babylonians have always been enemies of the Cross whether at war or for peace because of the idolatry. They did not serve the Most High. Therefore, having recently been delivered from Assyria, he should have been more cautious concerning those he allowed in his palace. As it is written, concerning details of the visitors, they seemed to come with good intentions. However, after being privileged to see what they did see in the house of the true and living God and all he provided and his many treasures, their intent changed. How godly can someone be if they don't serve the true and living God? How can they show the fruits of the spirit if they don't have the Spirit? Faithfulness, peace, ethics, and integrity along with discretion come with knowing God.

Sometimes we ourselves open doors for friendly fire by allowing people to see too much or speaking too much to someone that has no intention on being a part of the Kingdom of Righteousness. There are appointed times to share a testimony as led by His Spirit. There are other times where you may look back and realize that revealing certain things was an action of foolishness. In times past, we have done those things that didn't edify or build but brought forth self-inflicting because of choosing to share with the wrong person.

Though you may have good intentions because of your humility and wanting to boast somewhat in what the Lord has done, not all are Israel that came from Israel. Everyone is not on the same level of maturity to handle certain revelations with discretion even if they say they can. For this same reason did Jesus Christ bring forth his word with mystery and revealed himself by the Holy Spirit at his appointed time. He will not put more on us than we can bear.

Some people that you fellowship with may be wonderful, God-fearing, and loving individuals. However, there are others you may invite for dinner, and they get a glimpse of what the Lord has done for you and sometimes the intent changes. They may see the size of your home or how many vehicles you have and then opinions start to form. How did they get that? How did they afford that? Did they get that with church money?

Then sometimes they try to come up with reasons within themselves why you shouldn't live the way you live, or they make it a priority to pattern their life around yours. They want what you have. However, they don't know the testimony of the work that the Lord wrought with you on the potter's wheel to get you to that place. They don't want to go through what you've gone through, but they want the end result of what they see in you. That wasn't their original intent. That's what makes it friendly fire. Most encounters often start humble and innocent. So, you must guard your heart. Be an effective gatekeeper. Protect what the Lord has given you by his Spirit. I am not suggesting that you isolate yourself or keep secrets. I am, however, counseling that you yield to the Holy Spirit completely to discern the righteousness of his will.

USE IT OR LOSE IT

When in war, you're in survival mode, and you have to learn to use what you have. Not just some things, but everything. As it is in the flesh, so it is also in the Spirit. I can't seem to say this enough…you'll hear it again.

For the kingdom of heaven is as a man traveling into a far country, who called his own servants, and delivered unto them his goods. And unto one he gave five talents, to another two, and to another one; to every man according to several ability; and straightway took his journey.

Then he had received the five talents went and traded with the same and made them other five talents and likewise he that had received two, he also gained another two.

But he that had receive one went and digged in the earth and hid his Lord's money.

After a long time, the Lord of those servants cometh and receiveth with them.

And so, he that had received five talents came and brought other five talents, saying Lord, thou deliverest unto me five talents: behold, I have gained beside them five talents more.

His Lord said unto him, well done, thou good and faithful servant: thou hast been faithful over a few things, I will make thee ruler over many things: enter thou into the joy of the Lord.

Then he which had received two talents came and said, Lord, thou deliverest unto me two talents: behold, I have gained two other talents beside them.

His Lord said unto him, well done, thou good and faithful servant; thou hast been faithful over a few things, I will make thee ruler over many things: enter thou into the joy of the Lord.

Then he which had receive the one talent came and said, Lord, I knew thee that thou art a hard man, reaping where thou hast not sown, and gathering where thou hast not strawed:

And I was afraid and went and hid thy talent in the earth: Lo, there thou hast that is thine.

His Lord answered and said unto him, thou wicked and slothful servant, thou knewest that I reap where I sowed not, and gathered where I have not strawed: Thou oughtest therefore to have put money to the exchangers, and then at my coming I should have received my own with usury.

Take therefore the talent from him and give it unto him which hath ten talents. For unto everyone that hath not shall be taken even that which he hath and cast ye the unprofitable servant into outer darkness there shall be weeping and gnashing of teeth.   *Matthew25:14-30*

      In warfare, the point is to annihilate the enemy. To do so you must use all your weapons. In the natural sense, you need to use all of your gifts and talents. All of them contribute to your daily warfare, whether you believe it or not, and no weapon is too big! Use every weapon you have to spew the enemy.

      The Lord is telling us even here that He has blessed us all with gifts and talents. If you think of it in the spiritual aspect, they could be considered to be your different contributions to be used in spiritual war.

      See, in war throughout the world today, some people work as bomb experts, some are in charge of fueling, some are administrators, etc. well, the same goes for the use of the spiritual gifts and talents that we have been blessed with for the purposes of kingdom building. Some of you have been blessed with the ability to sing, some of you are awesome on computers, and believe it or not, these things that many may consider small things are really huge parts of kingdom building.

      Many of us need to clean out our closets, too. We have gifts that we don't use (or should I say that they are not used for the uplifting of the kingdom), along with other junk stuck in our spiritual closets, and yet, we still petition the Lord for more when there is no room to receive any of the things you're requesting. To be straightforward, we need to stop asking for a while and use what we have. I can't stress this enough. I believe that's one of the reasons the Lord said that when we pray, we should ask, "Give us this day our daily bread." You must be faithful over what you have been blessed with before asking for an increase.

      Visualize how it is in war. You cannot carry everything with you to war. In battle you only take the necessary, the essentials. Anything else will weigh you down and get in the way of your functioning at your fullest potential.

      As a soldier, you must be able to maneuver away from the enemy quickly and on occasions, not be seen. So, travel light. The Lord has provided us with all of the essentials needed to get through a day at war successfully. We must also be careful to use wisdom, knowledge, and understanding throughout our decision making, for it is crucial in the time of war.

Come unto me, all ye that labour and are heavy laden, and will give you rest.

Take my yoke upon you and learn of me; for I am meek and lowly in heart: and ye shall find rest unto your souls. For my yoke is easy, and my burden light.

Matthew 11:28-30

Being in war, day after day, is not an easy job. As we have witnessed with the two wars fought in Iraq and Afghanistan, they were extremely costly. I believe that this is a reason why the Lord says to "choose this day who you will serve." You don't want your labor to be in vain. If you've chosen Him, then you have to be about Him all the way. For He stated that the lukewarm He will spew out of his mouth. So, in the military aspect, you will be eliminated in the crossfire because you cannot keep running back and forth to the different sides on the battlefield. It's all or nothing, His way or no way. In this scripture, the Lord lets us know that those who labor for Him have a light burden. The battle is already won. He reigns in victory!

Do you remember the headlines about the airlines charging for additional baggage at the airport? They were charging additional fees for bags weighing over fifty pounds. Well, take a moment to visualize a soldier on the battlefield. They only carry the absolute necessities. As I spoke of before, anything additional could cost the soldier majorly. Soldiers must be able to crawl, duck, crab walk, and run quickly. These things are nearly impossible to perform with extra baggage. Carrying more than what's absolutely necessary can slow you down; it can wind up having you caught up as a prisoner of war, injured, or even killed. Can you see the correlation? This goes on daily because daily we are in spiritual war. This race is not a sprint, but a distance run. So, for this reason we must travel light, cast our cares upon the Lord, and He will give us rest, for we will definitely need it!

And let us not get weary in well doing; for in due season we shall reap if we faint not. *Galatians 6:9*

We must be good soldiers of the cross and stand firm on the promises of God. We must know the Word of God. He gives us reassurance in Revelation 2:2-3:

I know thy work, and thy labour, and thy patience, and how thou canst not bear them which are evil: and thou hast tried them which say they are apostles, and are not, and hast found them liars:

And hast borne, and hast patience, and for my names sake hast laboured and hast not fainted.

And in revelation 2:7:

He that hath an ear, let him hear what the Spirit of the Lord saith unto the churches; to him that overcometh will I give to eat of the tree of life which is in the midst of the paradise of God.

The Lord is even awesome at encouragement! When the war is almost over, when we've done all that we can do, He says, stand and see the salvation of the Lord. For He is the author and the finisher of our faith. We must walk in the footsteps of Paul, who stated, I have fought the good fight; I have finished my course...so pick up your weapons...and fight!

This refers to spiritual baggage as well. You must rid yourself of spiritual strongholds, which will interfere with your effectiveness on the battlefield. The chains have been broken, and freedom has been declared through Christ and Jesus. Again, I say, remember the privileges of salvation. Surrender it all to God and leave it there. Don't pick it up again.

1 Cor 12:4-7 & 11

Now there are diversities of gifts, but the same spirit. And there are differences of administrations, but the same Lord. And there are diversities of operations, but it is the same God which worketh all in all. But the manifestation of the Spirit is given to every man to profit withal. But all these worketh that one and the self-same Spirit, dividing to every man severally as he will.

We have been gifted for a purpose. We have been called for a purpose. We didn't choose him, but he first chose us and loved us. The spiritual warfare has its purpose. We are not fighting just to fight, but to know him and glorify him.

Ephesians 4:7-13

But unto every one of us is given grace according to the measure of the Gift of Christ. Wherefore he saith, when he ascended up on high, he led captivity captive and gave gifts unto men. (Now that he ascended, what is it but that he also descended first into the lower parts of the Earth? He that descended is the same also that ascended up far above all heavens, that he might fill all things).

And he gave some apostles, and some prophets, and some evangelists, and some pastors, and some teachers; for the perfecting of the saints, for the work of the ministry, for the edifying of the body of Christ: till we all come in the unity of the faith, and of the knowledge of the Son of God, unto a perfect man, unto the measure of the statured of the fulness of Christ.

We are all many members of one body. We have a call of duty to the Lord. The Lord says he has given Apostles, Prophets, Evangelists, Pastors, and Teachers. That's the five-fold ministry. We must walk worthy of the vocation wherein we are called. We are the husbandmen. The earth is the vineyard the Lord has ordained us to go forth and He gave gifts to all men.

One of the things discussed in the previous chapters concerning friendly fire is that we must stay mission minded. Though the Lord distributes gifts as he will, they are to be used for his glorification and the edification of the body. Some people tend to get a little godly jealous regarding the distribution of gifts and talents. The thing we must understand is that we have nothing except what we have been given by God. What the Lord has given, was given to effectively fulfil his will and purpose. We are not purposed to go on our own will or our own authority. So, we must utilize the gifts and talents appropriately. We mustn't hide our gifts and talents in the earth.

We must also use the gifts and talents for the purposes of righteousness, and not for the fulfilment of worldly uses. I have seen many people blessed by the Lord with the ability to sing. Their voices were beautiful. However, instead of using their voices to sing unto the Lord, they sang worldly songs that appealed to sensual and fleshly desires. Most often it was because to them it seemed more lucrative. The questions to ask is, what does it profit a man to gain the whole world and lose his soul? They tell themselves it's only for a little while and then a while turns to years. Meanwhile, sin gives birth to death. The wages of sin is death, but the gift of God is eternal life through Christ Jesus. That's burying talents in the earth.

Certain things are not edifying or helping to build the kingdom of the Most High. You must build the spirit man that craves the Spirit of God. We cannot allow ourselves to be concerned with why someone has been gifted one way and you've been gifted another. It's God's will by his Spirit that distributes how he pleases. Our ways aren't his ways, and our thoughts are not his thoughts. He has the ultimate plan for his body, His bride. We must maintain our role within the body, so we stay balanced. When you enter into a relationship with Christ, there are rights and there are responsibilities. The Lord Jesus Christ is very personal. He lets you know who he is to you and who he has designed you to be in him.

1 Cor 9:19-22

For though I be free from all men, yet have I made myself servant to all, that I might gain the more. And unto the Jews, I became as a Jew, that I might gain the Jews; to them that are under the law, as under the law, that I might gain them that are under the law; to them that are without law, as without law, (being without law to God, but under the law to Christ), that I might gain them that are without the law. To the weak became I as the weak, that I might gain the weak: I am made all things to all men that I might by all means save some.

    So, we can see that the Lord needs us to be who we need to be with the measure of gifts and talents that he has given us so that we may by all means necessary save some. Jesus shows this scripture goes for himself as well as us. He is stating that he will be who we need him to be in our lives and he expects us to be first partakers just as well and be all things to others so that they, too, will know Christ for who his is. He is a Father, he is a Brother, he is a Friend, he is a Healer, Deliverer, Savior, Refuge, Provider, Bridge, Rock, and the list continues for eternity.

    In previous chapters, we discussed knowing them that labor among you and we discussed humility. It is imperative that while being effective members of the Body of Christ that we recognize others that may have a gift that we do not have that they may be able to help perfect that which is lacking in the faith of another. An example is, if a prophet is given a word of wisdom or word of knowledge that reveals that someone was sick with an infirmity. They are being obedient to speak the Word of the Lord and generally, if the revelation is given by the prophet, it is for the purposes of edification and healing. Though the prophet spoke, it may be the Lord's will to use another member with the gift of healing or may intend to heal directly through their praise. Humility is important for the sake of righteousness and helping others get to their expected end in Christ Jesus. Nonetheless, the Lord Jesus has given all for the perfecting of the saints so that we all come into the unity of the faith and knowledge of God.

Let Go, Let God.

    When you're in the midst of spiritual battles you must lay aside every weight and sin, and put them at the feet of Jesus. In previous chapters, we mentioned about not leaving a man behind. However, in certain circumstances you leave a man when he absolutely refuses to come into the ark of safety. As a pastor, one of the toughest things I've had to do was walk away from someone who refused the life raft. There's nothing you can do. As one that is to be a gatekeeper it's heartbreaking to want someone to see and walk in a more excellent way in Christ, and they reject you. This is a life of predestination, so if they belong to the Lord, it may be ordained for someone else to come behind you later and sow more seeds into their life. Then, they come onboard. In other instances, there are tares and no matter what you do, they are not going to receive you. We cannot allow any form of rejection to be a burden. You must let go and let God have his way. When you have been stretched beyond measure to "by all means save some", it is then you must carry on. Stay the course. Remember, John 6:39 *and this is the father's will which hath sent me, that of all which he hath given me I should lose nothing, but should raise it up again at the last day.*

Forgiveness

It's hard to maneuver with weights you're carrying. This must be said matter-of-fact. Forgiveness is the very basis of us receiving salvation and it is conditional. We cannot be forgiven without forgiving others. We cannot hold onto things or "grudges", as another may call it. We must let go and let God handle the situations concerning us. This is the wisdom and fear of the Lord.

Matthew 18:21

Then came Peter to him, and said, Lord, how oft shall my brother sin against me, and I forgive him? Till seven times? Jesus said unto him, I say not unto thee, until seven times: but, until seventy times seven.

The cross is heavy. The point of Jesus dying on the cross for us was not to hold on to burdens, but with his death and resurrection came liberty and freedom from bondage. He stated that likewise we should deny ourselves and take up our cross. We cannot carry the cross alone. That's why he sent His Spirit, the Comforter.

We must allow the Holy Spirit to do his job of comfort while we release the burdens to Jesus and forgive those who have trespassed against us. Show mercy and compassion the same way Jesus has shown toward us. Forgiveness of a brother of sister, even who is not of Christ, is often easier said than done. It is easier to forgive someone who is repentant and godly sorrowful for their transgression.

It is not easy to let go when someone offends us and has no intention of changing. They have no regrets, and if given another opportunity they may even do it again. Thank God for Jesus Christ who forgave us our sins while we were yet in the midst of our sin. We must grasp the same concept. We wrestle not against flesh and blood. Sometimes, we don't know why people treat us the way they do. There is always some kind of spiritual force behind our trouble and suffering. Pick up your weapons and fight utilizing the blood of Jesus that will never lose its power. Use the cross to fight and the blood-stained banner of love and forgiveness. Love those that hate you without cause. Pray for those who despitefully use you.

We must fight with an overcoming spirit. The word states that those who endure unto the end shall be saved. He also stated that overcomers shall see God and he will give them to eat of the tree of life. There is so much for us to look forward to! While we are in the midst of overcoming, we must continue to give God the glory, with our praise. Remember, praise lifts the spirits of heaviness.

Loss, Grief, Death

When we talk about spiritual warfare and putting on the whole armor, we often get visuals of the guns and ammo; we think about swords and shields. However, what many cannot fathom is the casualties of war. With warfare there is much loss, grief, and death. Though we know of it and that it occurs, it is hard to grasp the concept until we experience it ourselves.

That is why it is so important to guard your heart and be an effective gatekeeper. You see death, you see destruction, you see the results of people failing to surrender to the will and purpose of Christ. Some of the end results are because people refused to stand firm and fight. We cannot take down our standards of righteousness. We cannot compromise. We cannot be concerned with outward appearance and emotions.

The Lord has warned his servants that as the earth continues to spin and get more evil, that we will see death. Some, to the Glory of God and some for Operations of the Spirit of God. With death sometimes there are questions of "Why did that happen at such a time as this?"

When experiencing the loss of a loved one or acquaintance, spiritual warfare doesn't cease because of mourning or grief. Truthfully, the enemy will attempt to gain advantage during such times, with attempts to bring depression, loneliness, and even doubt in our ability to overcome.

We must recognize that the wages of sin is death, but the gift of God is eternal life through Christ Jesus. If sin is abounding throughout the world then death is the result. The Lord has given us the Word and the Lord has given us the choice to abide in that Word. We respect the choices of others, yet we fear the Lord with a reverent fear. His Word will stand. So, we must be content with the Lord's will and what he has allowed because of the choice of some to surrender to the will of Christ and as well as for others who rejected the Love of Christ. Jesus is the one who died. Jesus rose. Jesus is on the right hand of God while his enemies are made his foot stool. We must not be sorrowful or be taken with sudden astonishment or bewildered. We must continue to allow the Holy Spirit to reign and be our guide. Keep seeking the Face of God. He is a rewarder of them that seek Him diligently. He is still a refuge. He is still a comforter.

When trouble or trials come or when dealing with loss, some go to the world for support and counsel. However, it is not the Lord's intent for the children of the true and living God to go to the world for answers only he can give. Counseling is given by the Spirit of God to those who are willing to receive the truth in his fullness. Again, I say we must eat the whole loaf. All of it. For Jesus Christ is the Bread of Life. He is here to comfort, to deliver, and set free prisoners that are bound. Be not weary in well doing. Keep fighting a good fight. You may cry out to the Lord sometimes, but don't stop trusting that Jesus loves you and you are fully persuaded that nothing can separate us from the Love of Christ. These things should be considered regarding any type of loss or grief.

Whether you've lost a child, experienced miscarriage, lost a relative, a home, or even a job. Regardless, of what the Lord has allowed to die in your life, we can ask the question, did it birth a righteous drive in you? Did it propel you into a higher expectation of the Lord's move of faith in your life? Did it press you to seek him that much more diligently? Did it push you to praise the Lord more for his mercy and compassion?

Psalms 126:5-6

They that sow in tears shall reap in joy. He that goeth forth and weepeth, bearing precious seed, shall doubtless come again with rejoicing bringing his sheaves with him.

To appoint unto them that mourn in Zion, to give unto them beauty for ashes, the oil of joy for mourning, the garment of praise for the Spirit of Righteousness, the planting of the Lord, that he might be glorified.

Him that is weak in the faith receive ye, but not to doubtful disputations.

We then that are strong ought to bear the infirmities of the weak and not to please ourselves. Rom 14:1 and Rom 15:1

In these two passages, the Lord Jesus mentions the weak that are in the faith, and he mentions the strong that are in the faith. While we have mentioned briefly some details regarding tragedies and wounds that sometimes we see while contending for the faith; there are times when such encounters devastate a person, and they take a beating to their faith.

Sometimes, there are babes in Christ that are on the battlefield and haven't established a strong enough encounter with Jesus and are still somewhat sensitive or weak in the faith. Remember the phrase "In the faith." Whatever the reason for the weakness, they are still in the faith. They are still believing on the name of Jesus Christ. The Lord instructs us to receive them, however, not to doubtful disputes. Meaning, that we will go forth in the faith believing that we are standing in righteousness.

We will respect the fact that many people are on different spiritual levels on their journey with the Lord. There are some who may not have received the revelation of Jesus Christ as you have received. They may not have supped with the Lord as often as you have or whatever the case may be. The Word asks the question through the Apostle Paul stating, "Are all Apostles? Are all Prophets? Are they all Hebrews?" We are called with different gifts and calls as well as personalities. Yet, we walk worthy of the vocation wherein we are called. The Word also instructed that the strong were to bear the infirmities of the weak. We are here to edify and build, perfect that which may be lacking in the faith. The cross is heavy. Sometimes we need help with giving our burdens to Jesus and carrying the cross.

There is another portion of the scripture that states for the strong to not please themselves. There are moments when you're in a position of strength that you see another brother or sister is a position of weakness on the battlefield. They are our responsibility. We must bear their infirmities until they're in a position to overcome. There are occasions where we're the EMT (Emergency Med Tech). We must do what needs to be done so they are not on spiritual life support, but that they are in a position to keep fighting and endure unto the end.

The flesh doesn't want to fight. The flesh is weak. The spirit is willing. We cannot please ourselves by leaving a soldier behind because you've got your own cross to bear… "That by all means we might save some." Sometimes you're stretched beyond measure for the sake of saving the soul of a brother of sister; that's the purified love of Christ. The overcomers shall see God. So, pick up your weapons and fight!

KILL IT ON CONTACT…RECOVER QUICKLY

Many of us have learned by now that part of the battle is in our mind. Oftentimes, I've said that the things that the enemy places in our mind are like roaches and flies. Those are two creations that many of us can't stand to be around. Not too long ago (years ago), there was a commercial which aired for a bug repellant called "Contact," and their motto, if I may recall, was, "Kill it on contact." So, I take that to mean that we should stop it at the very root, at the first foundations, immediately! I can reflect back on warmer months when the flies would come into the house because one of the children had left a door opened. My husband would stop whatever he was doing to kill that fly. It became an absolute priority. He had to "kill it on contact," before it laid eggs and we had bigger problems on our hands. So, the same goes for us Christians.

We cannot let our minds be a trash dump for the devil. We must "kill on contact" every filthy and nasty thought that the enemy puts in our head. He may put in our minds to cuss someone out and to go and tell them a thing or two about themselves. He may have us feeling insecure about ourselves as if we can't go on any further, like we don't matter. See, things start in our mind, and if we allow them to, they can grow into actions. We must stay spiritually aware and utilize all of our spiritual weapons of warfare that the Lord has given to us to nip things in the bud early. Things being in our mind is one thing, that's the original deposit, but when it transfers from the mind to the heart, then "Houston, we have a problem!" Our enemy's weapons of mass destruction have not been activated, but they have become effective at the point. "Kill it on contact!" We also must be careful and do what our parents oftentimes have told us, which is to "think before we speak" out of our mouths. Remember, our mouth is a powerful weapon. We must choose our words carefully.

Keep in mind that the enemy wants to have us, to sift us like wheat. His missions are to steal, kill, and destroy. We cannot afford to lose ground; we must stay the course. Have the courage and the strength to continue fighting, though you've been wounded. Have wisdom to know when to leave the battlefield temporarily for treatment. If you must leave the battlefield, recover quickly.

In the US Military, there is a saying: "Never leave a man behind." Well, it's the same in spiritual warfare. At the very least, it takes one man to carry another soldier off the battlefield. So, let's get a visual and do the math a moment. Say for instance, there are five thousand soldiers on the battlefield for Christ. One thousand of those soldiers get wounded while in battle. The wounds are severe and require treatment. So, for every wounded soldier, there is another soldier required to escort the soldier off to safety. So, two times one thousand is two thousand, right? Well, then that's two thousand soldiers who have left the battlefield for Christ, which leaves only three thousand remaining soldiers fighting on the battlefield for Christ. For this reason, we must kill on contact daily issues, circumstances, and situations we come in contact with, which the enemy uses as stumbling blocks to deter us from finishing the course and fighting the good fight. We must take a lickin' and keep on tickin'.

However, I understand that some wounds are more severe than others. If you must leave, recover quickly. See, warfare is not just about strategy. It's also about unity and obedience. The more soldiers we have in unity on the battlefield for Christ, the easier it will be to penetrate the walls of the enemy's defense and eliminate the effectiveness of his tactics. We must destroy the enemy's weapons of mass destruction. We must "kill it on contact."

A House Divided Cannot Stand

And Jesus knew their thoughts, and said unto them, every kingdom divided against itself is brought to desolation; and every city or house divided against itself shall not stand: and if Satan cast out Satan, he is divided against himself; how shall then his kingdom stand? And if I be Beelzebub cast out devils, by whom do your children cast them out? Therefore, they shall be your judges. But if I cast out devils by the Spirit of God, then the Kingdom of God is come unto you. Or else how can one enter into a strong man's house and spoil his goods, except he first bind the strong man? And then he will spoil his house. He that is not with me is against me; and he that gathereth no with me scattereth abroad.

Matthew 12:25-30

Wisdom builds the house. Wisdom states that where there is unity, there is strength. If the Lord Jesus desires the unity in the faith, then surely the enemy will attempt to divide and conquer. While Jesus Christ ministered in the earth, there were some that came and challenged the way he did things. Many are the afflictions of the righteous, but he delivers them out of them all. When you're righteous there will be adversaries wanting to weaken the hands of the saints. They know a house divided will fall. However, to divide one must weaken the strength of the bond of unity. With the situation with Jesus Christ the adversary tried to bring controversy and discord among those in the midst that had seen the signs, miracles, and wonders that were intended to strengthen and perfect that which was lacking in the faith. By his Spirit all things are possible. Where the Spirit of the Lord is there is liberty.

In verse 29, Jesus asks, "Or else how can one enter a strong man's house, and spoil his goods, except he first bind the strong man?"

We must receive the Holy Spirit so that we can walk in the unity of faith in Jesus Christ. Setting captives free is warfare. People aren't set free without some kind of wrestle. Yet, by His Spirit the captives are set free. However, the adversary comes to attempt to bind the strong man in attempt to bring down the house and scatter the flock.

The strong man is the Spirit of God. He must reign completely. He shouldn't be grieved or quenched. We must kill on contact the issues that the adversary comes with to bring chaos, turmoil, discord, and confusion. We know that God is not the author of such things and by entertaining these forces can lead you into division and ultimate destruction, if the Lord doesn't intervene. Yield to the Holy Spirit and you will not fulfil the lusts of the flesh!

Isaiah 59:1-2

Behold, the Lord's hand is not shortened, that it cannot save; neither his ear heavy, that it cannot hear:

But your iniquities have separated between you and your God and your sins have hid his face from you, that he will not hear.

There is no separation in Christ; meaning in repentance. Jesus paid the ransom with his blood so we can boldly come to his Throne of Grace and be washed clean of our sins and transgressions. Jesus came that we may have life and have it more abundantly. However, the adversary comes to bring sin and separation. He wants you to lose your promise and inheritance. That's what it means to destroy. The Lord has pleaded even by the mouth of his prophets to ask, is his hand shortened, that it cannot save? He is there waiting to answer the prayer of true repentance. He will hear. He will deliver. So, "Kill it on contact" anything that is contrary to the word of God. Jesus is about forgiveness and unity. That's the purified Love of Christ.

Ezra 4:1-5

Now when the adversaries of Judah and Benjamin heard that the children of the captivity builded the temple unto the Lord God of Israel, then they came to Zerubbabel, and to the chief of the fathers, and said unto them, let us build with you: for we seek your God, as ye do, and we do sacrifice unto him since the days of Esarhaddon, King of Assur, which brought us up hither. But

Zerubbabel, and Jeshua, and the rest of the chief of the fathers of Israel, said unto them, ye have nothing to do with us to build an house unto our God: but we ourselves together will build unto the Lord God of Israel, as King Cyrus, the King of Persia hath commanded us. Then the people of the land weakened the hands of the people of Judah and troubled them in building. And hired counselors against them to frustrate their purpose, all the days of Cyrus, King of Persia, even until the reign of Darius, the King of Persia.

Keep in mind, when you're walking in obedience to do the Lord's will and helping build the Kingdom of God, there will be adversaries who attempt to frustrate your purpose in Christ. The Lord had given instruction for his chosen, (though they had gone into captivity) to build the temple: isn't it interesting how no matter what situation or circumstance you're in that the Lord will still make a way for his mission to be accomplished? Even in the midst of captivity and in the presence of your enemies, he will make provision.

Their adversaries heard that the foundation had been laid and that the Children of Israel were starting to build the temple. So, they came and made request that they may build with them. Why? Why would an adversary want to help the Lord build? Many adversaries are present while the Lord is doing a work. He prepares a table before us in the presence of our enemies that he may be glorified. They had no true heart desiring to help them build. Some attempt to come a long and take credit for what the Lord has done. While others attempt to destroy from the inside, spying our liberties in Christ.

The children of Israel discerned the intent of the adversaries and advised that they would do the Lord's will themselves according to the Lord's will and purpose. As much as we may want others to help us build, it may not necessarily be the Lord's will. Sometimes, you'll see the true intent was not friendly anyhow.

The people of the land began to weaken the hands of the Children of Judah. Does that sound like a people who seek our God? The enemy desires to weary the Saints of God. We must stay the course. Jesus will not put more on us than we can bear, and he will not provoke his children to wrath.

The people of the land began to frustrate them and hinder the work of the Lord. However, the Lord has the final say. No weapon formed against us shall prosper. The account that the Lord gives in this scripture is concerning a temple built with man's hands. There was a resistance and warfare to delay the work. How much more so will we encounter building the Spiritual Kingdom that's not built with man's hands? We are building an everlasting kingdom. There is no conspiracy, utter, proclamation, or decree that can overcome the

Spirit of God. The work has already been done in the Spirit. It's been signed, sealed, and delivered. No matter the frustration or agitation the Lord's will shall come to pass. Trust in the Lord with your whole heart. Fret not thyself because of evildoers neither be envious of workers of iniquity. The Lord sees all and knows all. He reigns in victory.

Psalms 37:10

For yet a little while, and the wicked shall not be yea, thou shalt diligently consider his place, and it shall not be. But the meek shall inherit the earth; and shall delight themselves in the abundance of peace.

So, kill on contact any tactics the enemy attempts to use to frustrate you or attempts to have you to give up on walking in your purpose in Christ. Kill it on contact when the enemy uses his tares to frustrate your purpose. Know who you are in Christ. Speak the Word in season and out. Resist the Devil and he will flee. You're on a mission to help build the Kingdom of God and his Kingdom is an everlasting kingdom. There will surely be adversaries that will come with the intent to frustrate your purpose in Christ.

Matthew 5:11-12

Blessed are ye, when shall revile you, and persecute you, and shall say all manner of evil against you falsely, for my sake rejoice, and be exceedingly glad: for great is your reward in Heaven: for so persecuted they that the prophets were before you.

So, pick up your weapons and fight that you may obtain your Heavenly reward!

THE WARFARE

I returned and saw under the sun, that the race is not given to the swift, nor the battle to the strong...   *Ecclesiastes 9:11*

The race is never given to the swift, neither the battle to the strong, but those who endure to the end shall be saved. This race we are running, unfortunately, is not a sprint. For this reason, I believe the Lord makes it clear in the Scripture that sprinters are not given the race, neither are those who are strong because this race is a distance run and requires runners who are conditioned, who have stamina and endurance to finish to the very end. Our Lord gave us His Spirit to dwell with us while He is absent in the flesh. The Spirit He left us is not just a Comforter, but also a finisher. The Lord has always assured us that His Word does not return void, but that it accomplishes that which it was sent forth to accomplish.

When Jesus therefore had received the vinegar, he said it is finished and bowed His head, and gave up the ghost.   *John 19:30*

Even in the beginning, God was a finisher. In Genesis 2:1, it is written, "Thus the heavens and the earth were finished, and all the host of them." He is the same yesterday, today, and forever more. Notice that the reward and the benefits are always in completion, not the beginning or the middles, but the end. Even Paul stated, "I have fought the good fight, I have finished my course."

Anyone who has ever been in any type of battle or war and was sold out for the cause would say, "Win or lose, we must stay the course and carry it out to the end." The same goes for us in spiritual warfare. We must have the mentality, "For Jesus we live, for Jesus we die." Stand firm on a solid foundation of faith without wavering. Believe that Jesus indeed is the author and the finisher of our faith. Know why you're fighting and following through with the orders you've been given by your commanding officer, which is not only to save that which is lost, but to go forth with a no-fear-of-the-devil mentality.

God has not given us the Spirit of Fear. Understand that we will be tried by fire. However, know that the Lord is the Goldsmith. Besides being our commanding officer, He shaped the gold into its final product. Even gold in its purest form must be refined and put through fire to eliminate all the impurities.

The goldsmith always knows the right temperature for refining. It's never too hot! And get this, the gold never tells the goldsmith what to create, just as the clay never tells the potter what the potter should mold. Through fire, we as soldiers are made stronger. We learn how to use our weapons and become more proficient. It is through the fire that we build stamina and endurance. The Lord used the story of Shadrach, Meshach, and Abednego to reassure us that there is a reward for those who are finishers and endure.

If it be so, our God whom we serve is able to deliver us from the burning fiery furnace, and he will deliver us out of thine hand, O King.

But if not, be it known unto thee, O King, that we will not serve thy gods, nor worship the golden image which thou hast set up.

Then the King promoted Shadrach, Meshach, and Abednego in the province of Babylon. Daniel 3:17-18,30

There is always promotion when you stay the course that the Lord has set out for you, and you finish the race until the very end. Again, I say, stand firm on your foundation of faith, and do not waver. Know that the Lord is a deliverer and a present help in the time of trouble.

He answered and said, lo, I see four men loose, walking in the midst of the fire, and they have no hurt; and the form of the fourth is like the Son of God.

Daniel 3:25

He is with us always. We cannot wander around, going to and fro, looking for security and assistance from man. We must look to the hills from which cometh our help, knowing always that our help cometh from the Lord. It is not by our own strength or our own might that we are not consumed, but because the Lord is our Rock and Fortress, our strength and our Redeemer. Eye have not seen, nor ear hear, nor entereth the heart of man the thing which the Lord has prepared for them that love Him…we must finish!

To him that overcometh will I grant to sit with me in my throne, even as I also overcame, and am set down with my father in his throne.

He that hath an ear, let him hear what the Spirit saith unto the churches; To him that overcometh will I give to eat of the tree of life, which is in the midst of paradise of God. Rev 3:7

Know what lies in store for you at the finish line. Many of the best runners in the world compete for the Olympic Gold Medal; their drive and motivation is what gets them the prize. The Lord tells us that in His Father's house are many mansions; "I go to prepare a place for you. If it were not so, I would have told you…" Let me repeat that, "If it were not so, I would have told you!" Again, I say that God is not a man that He should lie, neither is He the Son of Man that He should repent. His Word does not return unto Him void, but it goes forth and accomplishes that which it was sent to accomplish. So, with this being yet another confirmation, let us press toward the mark for the prize of the High Calling, which is in Christ Jesus, Our Lord.

Keep Your Eyes On The Prize

1 Corinthians 9:23

And this I do for the Gospel's sake, that I might be partaker thereof with you. Know ye not that they which run in a race run all, but one receiveth the prize? So, run that ye may obtain. And every man that striveth for the mastery is temperate in all things. Now they do it to obtain a corruptible crown; but we an incorruptible. I therefore so run, not as uncertainly; so fight I not as one that beateth the air: but I keep under my body, and bring it into subjection: lest that by any means, when I have preached to others, I myself should be a cast away.

    The Apostle Peter gave the account of what happens when we focus on the wrong thing and take our eyes off the prize. When he recognized Jesus coming toward him, he desired to walk on water with Jesus, but when his focus shifted to the rough seas instead of walking with Jesus, Peter began to sink. He began to doubt.

    We cannot get caught in the cares of the world or things of this life. We are here to do a mission for the Lord and when the mission is accomplished, we return to our home on High that the Lord has prepared for us. Our hope is to obtain an incorruptible crown and in order to obtain we must keep the flesh under subjection and seek to fulfil our God-given purpose. These things we do that we also may be partakers and not be castaway.

John 14:12-15

Verily, Verily, I say unto you, he that believeth on me, the works that I do shall he do also; and greater works than these shall we do, because I go unto my father. And whatsoever ye shall ask in my name, that will I do, that the father may be glorified in the son. If ye shall ask anything in my name, I will do it. If ye love me, keep my commandments.

    The Lord Jesus Christ has given us a responsibility and missions which must be accomplished to whom much is given, much is required. He said that a greater work would we do. We, in our journey should be putting others in a position to take what we have done and do a greater work. When Jesus Christ came and set the standard for us, He equipped us with the ability to stand on his foundation to do an even greater work because he was going to live with the Father on High.

There are several key players that come together in unity to build a house. There are architects, carpenters, electricians, plumbers, and so on. When one role player has completed their portion of their project, then they give the authorization for another role player to pick up where they left off and do their job until the home is completed to the builder's specifications. Somewhat similar to that of a relay race. Each runner has a portion of the race to run and then must pass the baton so that the others on the team may complete the race.

Some have said, "It's not always how you start, but how you finish." We must have the intent on finishing the race and doing it with Jesus. We must let the Chief Cornerstone do his job, we must do our job, and we must yield to the Holy Spirit to do his job so the work is sealed and "built to code", as some would say. We want the father to say, "Well done, thy good and faithful servant."

Hebrews 3:1-6

Wherefore, holy brethren, partakers of the Heavenly calling, consider the apostle and high priest of our profession, Christ Jesus, who was faithful to him that appointed him, as also Moses was faithful in all his house. For this man was counted worthy of more glory than Moses, inasmuch as he who hath builded the house hath more honour than the house. For every house is builded by some man; but he that built all things is God. And Moses, verily, was faithful in all his house, as a servant, for a testimony of those things which were to be spoken after; but Christ, over his own house; whose house are we, if we hold fast the confidence and the rejoicing of the hope firm unto the end. So, in all that we do to fulfil the Lord's will, let us also remain faithful to the mission and see things through to the end.

Let us not be weary in well doing for we shall reap if we faint not. Trust in the Lord. Lean not unto your own understanding. Jesus Christ is the Chief Apostle and Master Carpenter worthy of all of the honor. We are his masterpiece. We, too, are a testimony of his work to compel others also to partake of the heavenly calling. As servants of the royal priesthood this is our profession. Let us do it faithfully, with confidence, and in the Spirit of Excellence.

1 Cor 15:58

Therefore, my brethren, be steadfast, unmoveable, always abounding in the work of the Lord, forasmuch as you know that you labor is not in vain in the Lord.

NO FEAR OF THE ENEMY

I know by now you've been reading and are probably wondering why I continue to include so much scripture, as if you don't have a Bible of your own. To answer your question, I must first reiterate how crafty the enemy is. I want to get around any distractions or anything that will have you put the book down. The enemy will have you believe that you will put the book down and pick it back up once you get home or when you get to a Bible. He may also conveniently have your boss tell you that you can't read your Bible while working, so like Ragu, "It's all in here."

So, with that out of the way, let's turn to 1 Samuel 17:32-38, which states:

And David said to Saul, let no man's heart fail because of him; thy servant will go and fight with this Philistine.

And Saul said to David, thou art not able to go against this Philistine to fight with him: for thou art but a youth, and he a man of war from his youth.

And David said unto Saul, thy servant kept his father's sheep, and there came a lion, and a bear, and took a lamb out of the flock:

And I went out after him, and some him, and delivered it out of his mouth: and when he arose against me, I caught him by his beard, and smote him, and slew him.

Thy servant slew both the lion and the bear: and this uncircumcised Philistine shall be as one of them, seeing he hath defied the armies of the living God.

David said moreover, The Lord that delivered me out of the paw of the lion, and out of the paw of the bear, he will deliver me out of the hand of this Philistine. And Saul said unto David go, and the Lord be with thee.

And Saul armed David with his armour, and he put a helmet of brass upon his head; also, he armed him with a coat of mail.

I'm sure many of you have heard the story of David and Goliath. However, I would like you to take a look using a different perspective. What does the story really reveal to you? When I first began in ministry, I oftentimes dealt one-on-one with the Spirit of Fear. I knew that being a pastor was an extremely serious position and required a great amount of responsibility. I was afraid for several reasons. I wondered if people would receive the Word from me with being a woman in ministry. I wondered if they would receive it being that I was young. I feared failure. I feared rejection by friends and family. This list can go on and on. However, the Lord told me to go forth with a no-fear-of-the-devil ministry. For God has not given us a Spirit of Fear, but of Power, Love, and a Sound Mind. The key word here is power. One thing that we must be reminded of is that it's not by our power or our strength or our might, but by power sent from on High, His Spirit. How great is that power! We oftentimes forget that it's not our power that heals, delivers, and sets free. No, its power of the Holy Ghost!

So, lets focus on King David for a moment. In verse 32 of the above passage, he begins to speak to Saul and tells Saul to let no man's heart be troubled because of the giant. Many times, we can get caught up with the Spirit of Fear because of the way things look on the outside. Many of us, I'm sure, have had encounters with giants in our lives, such as your parents, a court appearance, bills that are due, facing foreclosure, or even a job loss. However, we must face our giants without fear, hitting them head-on, knowing that we've been given power from on High, having faith that our God is truly a delivering God.

Many times, I have gotten into different situations, and I looked at the problem at a whole from the outside, and the devil was laughing because, while I was looking from the outside in, I was filled with fear. I should have been looking at what I had. I was equipped with Jesus, and I had been given spiritual authority of all things which was told to me in Genesis 1:26.

See, sometimes we have to change the angle at which we view things. Instead of looking solely at the problem, look at the solutions. Speak the Word of God out of your mouth, knowing that the Lord will not put more on you than you can bare. Utilize all of your spiritual weapons, and when you've done all that you can do, look to the hills which cometh your help. Stand still and see the salvation of the Lord.

In verse 33, Saul told David that he was not able to go against the giant. Why? Because he was young, and the Philistine had more experience and training than he did. That happens more now than ever before. People will sit on the sidelines who have a lot less faith than you and will tell you all the reasons why you should not tackle the giants you are facing in your life. Basically, they are working for the enemy without even knowing it. In this story we're studying David. Saul was skeptical of his youth. Note that the devil will try to tear you down regardless of what your age is. Whatever your age is, you will have giants you're going to have to face. You will have trials, tribulations, and all types of challenges. Knowing all of this, the Lord sends us power from on High to penetrate the offensive line of the enemy's army. We must go forward with no fear of the devil, knowing that Jesus is the author and the finisher of our faith.

There was a time in my life when I was overextended financially. I was working in the mortgage industry, and bank began to go down left and right. Well, eventually I lost my job, and frankly creditors could care less. They wanted their money. Looking from the outside in, this was a huge giant. I had children that I was responsible for, I need groceries, I needed the lights on and the water running. It wasn't the first day or even the first week that I realized how big this unemployment giant was. It was week two when the bills continued to come in, and I still had no clue of where I could work. I hadn't eve had an interview to get my hopes us; so, fear set in. However, I had to realize that real faith was the evidence of the things unseen. I had to see the unseen. I had to minister to myself, reciting that "The righteous shall not be forsaken nor his seed begging bread." He is a rewarder of those who diligently seek him. He is a provider, according to all of His riches in glory. If God be for me who can be against me? The Sword of the Spirit is a very comforting weapon to have.

In verse 34, David begins to remind Saul of the things which he had done in the past. He basically begins to share his testimony with Saul. He mentions that there was a time when he was keeping sheep that there came a lion and a bear to take the sheep out of the flock. That's how the devil sets us up when we have our minds made up the seek God and all of his righteousness. With us being the sheep, Satan will send not just a lion, but a bear also. How many times have you come home from having an awesome church service, great praise and worship, then the enemy sets you up for failure? Sometimes you can believe that you can get through anything if trials and test would come one at a time, but when they come two-by-two, hence the lion and the bear, we begin to raise questions, and the enemy stirs up doubt in our minds. We can get tossed to and fro, and even thrown off balance. That is why we must know who we are in Christ. We must utilize our spiritual weapons. We cannot be concerned about the giants that the enemy sends our way. We must press toward the mark for the prize and might of the Most High God and believe that the victory was won.

In verse 36, David then goes on to say that he slew both the lion and the bear. Then he speaks against the present giant (Goliath), who will also be conquered. This scripture reminds us that it's important to remember the Lord's track record—not just when it comes to other people's stories in the Bible, but also our very own testimonies and how He has brought us through many situations. We must go forth with no fear of the devil or any other unknown demonic forces, situations, or circumstances. We must bind the Spirit of Fear; for the Lord has stated in His Word that whatsoever is bound on earth is bound in heaven, and whatsoever is loosed on earth is loosed in heaven. So, we can loose power in the name of Jesus. We can loose love, joy, and peace. We can loose all of the fruits of the spirit. But we cannot do is be consumed with the Spirit of Fear. It's important to recognize the Spirit of Fear immediately and rebuke it. The enemy knows that he cannot come in through the front or the back door, so, he'll attempt to come in through the side with fear.

All of us have a job to do for the Lord, but if the enemy consumes us with fear, then guess what? Our work is not getting accomplished for the Lord because we're afraid to go forth and do it. If we're afraid of doing what the Lord has called us to do, then lives are not being saved and kingdom building is not being accomplished like it should, and therefore, the enemy has succeeded in doing his job, in some cases without you even knowing it.

In verse 37, David goes on, telling Saul that the Lord will deliver him out of the hand of the giant. Notice that he spoke it out of his mouth as a person of holy boldness and authority. He said it, and it was so without fear and without doubt. Using the Sword of the Spirit, which is the Word of God, will have our enemies flee and give us the ability to enjoy the green pastures on the other side of our mountains; knowing that there is nothing too hard for God, believing only that He is able to do all things but fail.

In verse 38, Saul is convinced by David that he is fit for battle. The only thing is that Saul gives David is his armor and when he tries it on, it doesn't fit. We spoke of this in chapter one. However, looking in a different revelation the same thing oftentimes happens to us. We begin to talk to friends, family, and those people in our inner circle when we are facing these giants in our life, and we talk about our different strategies, but they still attempt to equip us with their armor. They begin to tell us how they would handle things.

I remember when I had to go to court, and my family members gave me their share of opinions on what I should say to the judge. They armed me with their ideas. However, their armor wasn't for me. What God has for you, it is for you, and what God has for me, it is for me. We must do things God's way. The Lord will always equip you with the proper armor for every situation, circumstance, trial, or tribulation. It's up to you, however, to use it. The same goes for the Word of God and all the other spiritual weapons the Lord gives you. Application is extremely important.

See, we can't be hearers only, but both hearers and doers of the Word. We cannot be ever so learning and never coming to the full knowledge of the truth. Oftentimes, we can get spiritually lazy! We hear and hear and hear all these things and different stories about the Lord and how He hasn't given us the Spirit of Fear and all those other great sermons, but we must follow through with what he has taught us and apply it to our life. See, when David said he was going to fight the Philistine, he didn't just talk about what he was going to do, but he did what he said he was going to do! In this story, he wasn't a hypocrite who said one thing and did another. Keep in mind faith without works is dead. We spoke of this in previous chapters. God will do the impossible when we first do what is possible. Last, I want to mention a scripture in Jeremiah 1:5, 8-9:

Before I formed thee in the belly, I knew thee; and before thou camest forth out of the womb I sanctified thee, and I ordained thee a prophet unto the nations.

Be not afraid of their faces: for I am with thee to deliver thee saith the Lord.

Then the Lord put forth His hand and touched my mouth. And the Lord said unto me, behold I have put my words in thy mouth.

These scriptures really helped me when it came down to dealing with fear and all sorts of spiritual wickedness and principalities in high places. There were times when I had direct encounters with demonic forces with the names Hate, Murder, Kill, Secret, and the list goes on. These spirits were very strong, and when they came against my family and I, my most natural instinct was to run because of fear. However, I had to minister to myself with the Word of God. I couldn't fear the unknown. This is real faith, believing in the unseen, trusting solely in Jesus, knowing that He will never leave us or forsake us. I couldn't be afraid of the faces, both in the flesh and in the spirit (they looked horrifying) that came against me as I spoke the Word. I had to remember that before the foundations of the world, I was called and sanctified. I had to know that His ways are higher than my ways and His thoughts higher than my thoughts. I had to believe that there was a master plan and that I would overcome if I would first cast out all fears and believe that, through Christ, the battle was already won. Perfect love casts out all fear.

There was another situation I found myself in where I had a great deal of fear. I made mention of it briefly in the beginning of the book. I was attending a local church. At the time, I had already been ordained as a pastor. I recently relocated to the area, and I had yet to secure a building. So, I figured I would visit the church and indulge in the praise and worship until we got settled in the area as a ministry. Over a matter of weeks, my husband and I began to notice a conflict in the way they operated versus what the Word of God said. We decided it would be best to leave. The apostle and a few other members began to pray against us. I was afraid because of the power they had. They had the indwelling of the Holy Ghost, but they were not using their power according to the will of God. My fear also existed because I was being opposed by an apostle. I also was afraid that the Lord would allow them to overpower me. So, in that case I felt it was a situation of who had more power. However, when we're obedient and righteous in the sight of God, we must understand that it's not by our power or might but by the Spirit of God that all things exist. When we've done all that we can do, we must stand and see the salvation of God.

As a member of the armed forces one can admit that there are somehow times when fear may creep in, especially in a time of war. More specifically there is fear of the unknown that can play on your mind. You never really know if you're going to get bombed while riding up the road or if you're going to drive over an explosive device. There are numerous things that can go wrong. When things tend to be out of our control, it is a characteristic of the flesh for fear to set in. However, God stated that He did not give us the Spirit of Fear, and true faith must remain at the forefront of our lives in order to make it through.

Some of the ways we have been able to eliminate some of the "unknowns" in our military are through intelligence operations, which gather pertinent information in reference to our enemies and report back to us. Several members of our military operate in this role regardless of which branch of service. This confirms the Word given that we are many members but one body (1 Corinthians 12:20). In a spiritual sense, the main retriever and provider of most all of our spiritual military intelligence is the Holy Spirit.

The eyes of the Lord are in every place beholding both evil and good.

But ye have an unction from the Holy One, and ye know all these things.

As for thee, O king, thy thoughts came into thy mind upon thy bed, what should come to pass here after: and He that revealeth secrets maketh known to thee what shall come to poss.

Spiritual warfare takes place even amongst those who do not necessarily claim to be Christians. Nonetheless, if you keep your armor on at all times, you'll be able to see your enemies from afar. In the wars and battles we fight we must keep in mind that our lives and the lives of others depend on our obedience.

Personally, I've been blessed not to have fought in Desert Storm, Vietnam, or any other war on the natural battle ground. However, those who have will tell you that fear will often set in, but when you think of your lives and the freedom that you're fighting for, that fear is set aside and replaced with faith and courage. As Paul reminds us, we decrease, that the Lord may increase. So, lay aside every weight, including fear, and pick up your weapons and fight. We need you on the battlefield!

The Lord Jesus Christ has revealed many things thus far regarding spiritual warfare and His overcoming power. We know the mission and why we are fighting. Jesus has also shared the need to be a spiritual minded and disciplined soldier to be victorious. However, one of the subjects that we have not explored in depth are the tactics of fear and intimidation used by the adversary to get us as soldiers to retreat or wave the flag of surrender.

We cannot fathom the power that comes with being in unity with Jesus Christ by his Spirit. The enemy trembles when we're in line with the Word of God in confidence. He must flee! Because of the power and authority, we carry with faith and the Holy Spirit, our enemies will not approach through the front or back door, figuratively speaking. The enemy will use fear and intimidation, common methods of deception to put you on the run or back you in a corner. The Lord Jesus Christ has given us an arsenal full of our weapons to fight a good fight and walk in victory over our enemies and over sin. Our adversaries don't want us to use our weapons to defeat them. So, they use deception to get you to take down or compromise. Don't take down your standards of righteousness. Do not compromise with the adversary.

You're Not Ready/Qualified (a common deceptive tactic)

We all have tests and trials for the increasing of our faith. Some trials seem greater than others, sometimes seeming like our breakthrough is farther than we can fathom. Yet, we grow leaps and bounds and overcome.

One appointed time in my life when I was weaker in the faith, I was a pastor in my youth, and I started walking in my calling, and praying for the sick, and teaching the Gospel. I had no clue of the opposition I would face simply because of my obedience to do the will and purpose of Christ. I just went forth and did what the Spirit of God led me to do. People were healed, delivered, and set free. Lives were changed for the good. While these works of faith continued to manifest, the adversary used people who were of the Christian sector to intimidate us into quitting.

When I received an unction from the Lord Jesus to go forth and do a work, I didn't come out of a church organization. I hadn't been a deaconess for ten years, or an assistant pastor who served up the ranking for some big bishop. There wasn't this great ordination service. I simply answered the Voice of God.

So, the form of intimidation that other pastors, apostles, and many people used was to say that I was out of order. They said God does things in decency and in order, that I needed an apostle, and I needed a church building. They even went so far to say that women weren't pastors and that I was outside the will of God. Meanwhile, I just knew that I loved the Lord and I wanted to please him. I didn't often guard my heart in those situations and because of it I often cried to the Lord. I couldn't grasp the concept of how many people could say that they loved the Lord God, and those same people could put so many restrictions on that love and the power of God that accompanied such a love. During those times the Lord would minister to my Spirit and let me know that he was with me no matter the circumstance and no matter the situation. I didn't have very many opportunities to fellowship, but the signs, miracles, and wonders that he used me to do were beyond the walls of the church, just as the days of old. Nonetheless, the work and His will were still accomplished. There were often times of discouragement and even moments of full-blown anger, but I didn't give up, we kept trusting, seeking, and persevered through it.

You're Lost Already (another common form of deception)

There was an appointed time when I had been doing a great bit of work in the ministry, more actively than usual. I had consented to some speaking engagements and because of that I had more contact with demonic forces. There were some ministries I ministered within and yet when I refused to come in league with them and become a minister under them, all hell broke loose on my life. I subjected myself to a major spiritual attack which originated from a simple "yes" to a speaking engagement.

As much as we love the Lord Jesus, we must be certain that our ministering no matter the form, is according to his will and not our own. You can say no. Don't be afraid to say no. While I was under siege by those demonic forces, they were so strong and powerful. It was terrible. Those demonic forces that I encountered knew my strengths and my weaknesses. They brought up nearly all of the wrongs of my past, my short comings. They told me my works of righteousness had been done in vain. My husband didn't really love me or understand me. They told me I ministered to people too harshly the times I told them to repent. I abused my authority. Jesus didn't want me anymore. His Spirit had left because I should have had a covering.

Nearly within the same time frame my biological father had become ill and passed away. There was a play on my emotions and the love that I had for my dad. "If you loved him, you would have prayed more. You prayed, the Lord didn't answer. You didn't have the power like you used to. Since your natural father is gone, your spiritual father left also. You're a vagabond. You're a heathen. You're a bastard."

Those fiery darts kept coming back-to-back with guilt and all sorts of falsehood. When I was in the midst of this battle it was a struggle to overcome the strongholds. I had to fight. I had to praise. I had to overcome. I was fighting for my own life while responsible for being the gatekeeper for the souls of others. I was almost convinced that Jesus had forsaken me and that I was lost and destined for the pit of Hell. Someone on the outside looking in would wonder how one could think such things. The spiritual warfare is real. The devastation is real. The battle for redemptions and salvation is real. This is not for entertainment. Jesus Christ is not a myth. His Holy Spirit is real. The enemy used the tactic of deception so that I wouldn't put on my whole armor.

Some days I was convinced after not hearing the voice of God for some time, that he really did leave. There were days I didn't praise, I said, "What's the point, he's not listening?" All this happened because of me. It's my fault", I said to myself. However, thank God for his grace and his mercy as well as his longsuffering and compassion. The more I allowed the adversary to keep shooting those fiery darts and hesitating to speak the Word of God into the atmosphere, the longer it took me to overcome and get back on the battlefield for Christ. The prayers of the righteous surely availeth much. I am a living testimony of that fact. Jesus Christ gives us choices. We must let him reign completely. I must admit that there have been several times I put some of my armor down and it caused injury and could have possibly caused casualties. I'm also grateful that the Lord gives angels charge over us to handle those battles in the spiritual realm that we don't have strength to fight. Jesus will never leave you. He will never forsake you. Hold onto his hand and if you don't have strength to do anything else, open your mouth and call on the name of Jesus.

II Tim 1:7-8

For God hath not given us the spirit of fear, but of power, and of love, and a sound mind. Be not thou therefore ashamed of the testimony of our Lord, nor of me his prisoner: but thou partaker of the afflictions of the Gospel, according to the power of God.

Clearly, the Lord does not want us to be fearful. The Word states that with fear is torment. He doesn't want us tormented. He has given us the power that comes with love and a sound mind. All three are in a package. Though, we maintain reverent fear of the Lord Jesus Christ, he doesn't want us to be afraid or intimidated.

There is power that comes with faith in the Most High. The more faith you have, the more power you have to move in that faith. Therefore, be not ashamed of the testimony that the Lord Jesus is establishing in you. There will be many afflictions because of the Gospel wherein we are partakers. However, we walk in the power of God with the purified love of Christ. The Lord stated that he gave the Spirit of Power, Love, and a Sound Mind. The adversary will attempt to affect those three with the Spirit of Fear.

Fear can affect your soundness of mind, if you allow it. Remember, we must kill on contact those things which affect our mind of Christ. Fear, when entertained can make a person act crazy and irrational. Without the soundness of mind, you can react to situations with poor judgement which could potentially have your good evil spoken of. Let the spirit of a sound mind and purified love of Christ cast out all fear. With those three you can do all things through Christ that strengthens you and overcome. No matter what type of fear and intimidation the adversary shoots toward you, stand in the truth. In the moment of truth, you must ask yourself, "Will you remain faithful to the Most High?' He is the author and the finisher of your faith. Don't take down because of doubt, fear, deception, or intimidation. The overcomers shall see God. Stayed armed and dangerous! Pick up your weapons and contend for the faith.

THE POWER OF GOD

I have learned in the Word of God that Jesus was crucified for our sins and that on the third day He rose again with the keys of death and all power in His hand. This power and authority He has given to us also. Simply put, the power is in His Spirit. You must have the indwelling of the Holy Ghost to have effective power. In His Spirit is the power to heal, deliver, set free, work miracles, signs, and other wonders. How do we obtain this power? The power comes with the belief. You must believe in God's son Jesus Christ. There is no other way. Along with this belief, the power is received through the laying on of hands, fasting, prayer, and/or tarrying to name a few.

Verily, verily, I say unto you, He that believeth on me, the works that I do shall he do also; and greater works than these will he do; because I go unto my father.

And whatsoever ye shall ask in my name, that I will do, that the father may be glorified in the son. John 14:12-13

So, as long as we believe, then we can do the works of Jesus and even greater. However, the kicker is that we must believe, without doubt. The more we believe, the more power we will have.

And it shall come to pass that in the last days, saith God, I will pour out my Spirit upon all flesh: and your sons and daughters shall prophesy, and your young men shall see visions, and your old men shall dream dreams.

And on my servants and on my handmaidens, I will pour out in those days of my spirit; and they shall prophesy:

And I will shew wonders in the heavens above, and signs in the earth beneath; blood, and fire, and vapor of smoke. Joel 2:28-30

This tells me that with his power many will possess the ability to prophesy, dream dreams, and will also be given visions. Naturally if the Lord gives us these things, he will also bless us with the interpretation as well, whether through you or someone else. My, My, MY, what power this is! This is life-changing! The prophetic can be past, present, and the future. It gives confirmations, instruction, direction, and so much more. The enemy doesn't want us to know what our future holds and that all we've been through is for the glory of God.

The Bible tells us that without vision man will perish. So, through this His Spirit is the power to sustain. This power influences God's people to surrender their hearts, turn from their wicked ways, and walk uprightly before Him and gives the vision to see the success that lies ahead. When the Spirit of God is released upon His people, healing and deliverance takes place. This means that those suppressed, oppressed, and depressed by demonic forces have been freed. Satan has been defeated. The victory is won!

Not too long ago, I happened to be in the kitchen cooking breakfast when suddenly a representative came and cut off my electricity. My power had been shut off! The first thing I thought was, "Lord, what are your trying to tell me?" It couldn't have been a faith issue because in my heart I felt so far beyond that. I didn't believe the situation would make or break my faith at all. I was just somewhat angry and annoyed because I knew the bill had been paid and I had two young children to care for. Everything had stopped. I couldn't cook. I couldn't wash clothes. I had a mind to call and fuss out the electric company, but I had a cordless phone that needed electricity to function. I was upset with my husband because I told him we should have a generator, and the list goes on. I couldn't do any ministry work. My podcast studio for making broadcasts was inoperable. Finally, I said, "Come on, Lord. Today? Really? What are you trying to tell me?" He answered, "Work while it's day because when night falls, no man can work." Nothing gets accomplished without the operation of His Spirit. No healing, no deliverance, no miracles, etc. I laughed and said, "Lord, thank you, but I'm sure there were other ways you could have shared this with me." Stay spiritually connected to your source of power. Use your weapons and fight the enemy with all you've got.

On the flipside in the natural, our government has several branches of power. The executive, legislative, and judicial branches of government power are set in place to be sure that proper laws are originated and adhered to. We set standards and boundaries. When these lines are crossed by enemies both foreign and domestic, we may decide to take action, which sometimes can only be rectified through warfare. Then, the orders are issued accordingly to our troops through the powers that be.

What are you waiting for? We have the upper hand. We've been given power and domination over ever serpent, principality, and all rulers of darkness. We were created in the image of God. So, let's walk like Him and use the power God has given us to fight effectively on the battlefield for Christ. The beautiful thing is we never run out of power as long as we believe. Pick up your weapons and fight!

Have You Received Since You Believed?

One of the most powerful weapons of warfare to have in your arsenal is the Power of God, which is the Holy Spirit. You must have the indwelling of the Holy Spirit to survive and be kept with God. Within the Holy Spirit is the healing, signs, miracles, wonders all take place by His Spirit. Within His Spirit is your prayer language to speak with Jesus Christ. His Holy Spirit makes all things possible.

Acts 19:1-2

And it came to pass, that, while Apollos was at Corinth, Paul having passed through the upper coasts came To Ephesus: and finding certain disciples, he said unto them, have ye received the Holy Ghost since ye believed? And they said unto him, we have not so much as heard whether there be any Holy Ghost.

The Lord Jesus desired for us to be baptized with water as well as with the Holy Ghost and his refining fire. He said he was going to prepare a place for us and that he would leave us a comforter which is His Spirit. His Spirit is the Power of God and is connected with our faith and belief in him. The more faith we have in Jesus Christ, the more faith we have for the Spirit of God to operate in a situation. The signs will follow the believer.

Matthew 7:7-8

Ask, and it shall be given you; seek, and ye shall find; knock and the door shall be opened unto you: for everyone that asketh receiveth; and he that seeketh findeth; and to him that knocketh it shall be opened.

If you want to know how to be in complete unity with Jesus Christ, you must receive His Spirit, and all you have to do is ask for him. He is a gentleman and will simply tug a little at your heart but will not force himself. He gives the options.

To receive His Spirit, I must say that sometimes to lose is really to gain. Meaning, that you must lose yourself completely in him. Sometimes you must fast and pray to get out of the flesh so, that His Holy Spirit can break forth. In other instances, you can praise the Lord with your whole heart until his Spirit starts to overflow. The Lord pours out His Spirit in diversities of ways. Through him all things are possible. He eliminated the excuses.

Luke 9:1-2 & 10:19-20

Then he called his twelve disciples together, and gave them power and authority over all devils, and the cure diseases. And he sent them to preach the Kingdom of God, and to heal the sick.

Behold, I give unto you power to tread on serpents and scorpions, and over all the power of the enemy: and nothing shall by any means hurt you. Notwithstanding in this rejoice not, that the spirits are subject unto you; but rather rejoice, because your names are written in Heaven.

    Jesus Christ loved us so much that when he called us, he fully equipped us with the power we needed to fulfil the mission and purpose. Jesus knew before the foundations were created what he would purpose us to do. He also knew what we would be up against and what we needed to overcome. All things have been created for him and by him.

    There is an order to the Lord's purpose of things. He does things in decency and in order. You can say, "There's a method to the madness." He went to prepare a place for us and stated that a greater work would we do while he went to be with his father. He also stated that he would not leave us comfortless. The Comforter he would send to us on his behalf, which is His Spirit.

    The Lord gave us his power to overcome devils and cure diseases. He shares this in His Word so that we can understand some things that we will encounter in spiritual battle. The enemy will attempt to fight us with sickness and diseases as well as various tactics to bring fear, intimidation, and to weaken our faith. The Lord Jesus makes it clear that the spirits are subject to us. He then encourages us to rejoice because regardless of what happens in the midst of this earthly body, nothing that they do can hurt your soul. So, we can rejoice because our names are written in the Heavenlies. The Lord also reveals to us that he has given us power over serpents and scorpions. Those two types of creatures are designed with the intent to kill their victims and their bites or stings attempt to render their victims powerless and incapable of fighting back. Jesus, on the other hand says, he gave us the power over all power of the enemy! He didn't say, "Some", he said, "All."

    Knowing is merely a piece of the battle. We must not be slothful in the Lord's business. We must pick up our weapons that the Lord has equipped us with to fight. Though the battle really isn't ours to fight, the battle belongs to the Lord. Yet, it's by faith we stand. With our faith we move God and the angels he's given charge over us to fight on our behalf. There's a saying misery loves company. The Devil is a liar and has been from the beginning. His destination is the lake of fire. He has lost his Heavenly abode and wants you to lose your inheritance as well. For this reason, the Lord specifies for us to rejoice that our names are written in Heaven because that is a great piece of what the warfare is about…our residence with Jesus.

We Must Cherish Him

      The Power of God is our marriage to the Lord Jesus Christ. His Spirit signifies us partaking of the unity by the faith in him. The indwelling of His Spirit makes the bride of the Lord Jesus Christ of whom he is coming back for. We must cherish such a gift. He is truly our exceedingly great reward. Recognizing him as a gentle man and the guide of our lives, we must maintain the unity and yield completely to His Spirit. His Spirit has a rhythm, and we must maintain synchrony with His Spirit, so our actions are in his perfect timing.

      The Power of the Holy Ghost is special. He is a gift. The Lord stated in His Word that the wages of sin is death, but the gift of God is eternal life through Christ Jesus (Rom 6:23). That gift is his precious Spirit. His Spirit is not to be misused or played with. He commanded us to occupy until he comes. That means, while we wait, we are still responsible to go forth with works of faith, building the Kingdom of God because His kingdom is an everlasting kingdom. He is coming for a church that is without spot or wrinkle. Because of the gift of His Spirit we are able to be kept and maintain sanctification and holiness unto him. He said "Be ye holy, for I am holy." His Spirit and his refining fire are what allows us to walk in his holiness.

Psalms 24:3-4

Who shall ascend in the hill of the Lord? Or who shall stand in his Holy Place? He that hath clean hands, and a pure heart; who hath not lifted up his soul unto vanity, nor sworn deceitfully.

      His Holy Spirit cleanses so that we are able to stand and walk before him. So, cherish the gift of God as your exceedingly great reward. Yield completely to the will of His Spirit and relinquish your own will so that you are complete. His Spirit is what takes us places that we need to be so that healings take place and his other works of righteousness. His Holy Spirit is what takes us from earth to glory. By His Spirit we are able to maintain humility.

Philippians 2:5-10

Let this mind be in you, which was also in Christ Jesus: who, being in the form of God, thought it not robbery to be equal with God. But made himself of no reputation, and took upon him the form of a servant, and was made in the likeness of men: and being found in fashion as a man, he humbled himself, and became obedient unto death, even the death of the cross. Wherefore God also hath highly exalted him and given him a name of Jesus. Every knee shall bow, of things in Heaven, and things in earth, and things under the earth;

It is nothing we have done. Jesus counted us worthy as sons and daughters to partake of His Spirit. We, too, must not count it robbery to be equal by His Spirit, but rather cherish the unity given thereby. In His Spirit, we must follow hard after him; taking up our cross and denying ourselves. We ought not love our own lives, but walk in obedience even unto death. So, endure hardship as a good soldier. The overcomers shall see God and glorify his name. Stand tall and endure to the end.

POWER IN ~~NUMBERS~~...OBEDIENCE

Naturally, you know that the more people you have fighting for a cause, the more effective you are at conquering your enemies in battle in a timely fashion with minimal casualties. There is indeed power in unity, both great and small...

And did not he make one? Yet had he the residue of the spirit. And wherefore one? That he might seek a godly seed. Therefore take heed to you spirit, and let none deal treacherously against the wife of his young.

Malachi 2:15

In this particular scripture, I would like to focus on the fact that the Lord speaks expressly about seeking a godly seed. For this reason, I believe the Lord said on more than one occasion, be fruitful and multiply. Of course, he says this for more reasons than one. We can get numerous revelations from these scriptures; however, in this instance, being focused on spiritual warfare, we must realize that it requires a godly seed to fight in the Lord's army against Satan's empire. Of course, the more numerous we are, the more effective we become in unity.

In the society we live in today, many people tend to frown their faces at having many children. Some may try to stay within a comfort zone of one to two children. Of course, we've seen families having more children, but if you ask them, they will tell you that the children definitely weren't planned. I think to myself, you may not have planned it, but God always has a master plan. Bear with me. I'm going somewhere with this. Nowadays, we don't have children in the plan because we say we can't afford it, or we are more focused on ourselves and our careers. Where is your faith? My God is a provider according to all his riches in glory. However, we are not remotely concerned oftentimes (the majority of us) about what the Lord wants for us. We don't think to ask God what His plan is and make an attempt to do things God's way. Most of us lean toward our own understanding, and we allow our flesh to guide us in our decision-making process. When in fact, it was in the Lord's plan that we be fruitful and multiply, producing godly seeds, not just to be blessings unto you, not to create more bills for you, but to glorify God and to build up his kingdom. How can we expect to win in spiritual warfare if we are not recruiting and replenishing our soldiers? Never thought of it that way? Well, the enemy has! For the many of you reading, it's not too late to get started on those godly seeds (smile). Keep in mind, obedience is better than sacrifice.

The Lord has made numerous examples of how powerful numbers can be, throughout the reign of King David in particular. David has shown how if you seek the face of God and His righteousness, all other things will be added unto you. Many of you reading may already know that David was a man after God's own heart. Because he made doing the will of God his priority, he was blessed beyond measure. He is a prime example of the scripture," He is a rewarder of those that diligently seek Him." So, let's dive into one scripture in particular regarding King David when he numbered the people in 2 Samuel 24:1-10:

And again the anger of the Lord was kindled against Israel and he moved David against them to say, Go, number Israel and Judah.

For the king said to Joab the captain of the host, which was with him, Go now through all the tribes of Israel, from Dan even to Beersheba, and number ye the people, that I may know the number of the people.

And Joab said unto the king, Now the Lord thy God add unto the people, how many soever they be an hundredfold, and that the eyes of my Lord the king may see it: but why doth my lord the king delight in this thing?

Notwithstanding the king's word prevailed against Joab, and against the captains of the host. And Joab and the captains of the host went out from the presence of the king, to number the people of Israel.

And they passed over Jordan, and pitched in Aroer, on the right side of the city that lieth in the midst of the river of Gad and toward Jazer:

Then they came to Gilead, and to the land of Tahtimhodshi; and they came to Danjaan and about to Zidon,

And came to the stronghold of Tyre, and to all the cities of the Hivites, and of the Canaanites: and they went out to south of Judah, even to Beersheba.

So when they had gone through all the land, they came to Jerusalem at the end of nine months and twenty days.

And Joab gave up the sum of the number of the people unto the king: and there were in Israel eight hundred thousand valiant men that drew the sword; and the men of Judah were five hundred thousand men.

And David's heart smote him after that he had numbered the people. And David said unto the Lord, I have sinned greatly in that I have done: and now, I beseech thee, O Lord, take away the iniquity of thy servant; for I have done foolishly:

In this passage of scripture, David sends his captains out to number the people. The reason I'm using this example is to show King David's mind frame. We want to make sure that throughout all of our endeavors, we are giving credit where credit is due. We must recognize that the Lord is our strength and our redeemer and that nothing we do and prosper in is done in our own strength and power.

In these scriptures, David's captains try to remind him of these things and that all he has accomplished was because of the Lord. In verse three, Joab tries to bring King David down from the high horse he was on and says, "The Lord add to the people whatever number necessary, and whatever you need be. The Lord will provide, even as He has done so unto this point." However, David does not heed to the voice of his captain, and it is not until the count of the overall people comes back at 1.3 million that David's heart is softened unto repentance.

When you get the opportunity, go in and read about this in its fullness. In this particular chapter, for the sake of this lesson, look at all the people that David had been blessed with. Remember, we are talking about godly seeds and power in unity and obedience. The Lord added to him in numbers greater than he could have imagined.

Though King David had short comings, he was blessed because God was the head of his life. Because he was blessed, his people were blessed, and his peoples' people were blessed. We are not focusing on the consequence he had to pay; we're only focusing on the multitudes of hosts.

Now let's look at another situation where the Lord shows how great he is even while using small numbers. Reference Judges 7:1-7.

Then Jerubbaal, who is Gideon, and all the people that were with him rose up early and pitched beside the well of Harod: so that the Midianites were on the north side of them, by the hill of Moreh, in the valley.

And the Lord said unto Gideon, the people that are with thee are too many for me to give the Midianites into their hands, lest Israel vaunt themselves against me, saying, mine own hand hath saved me.

Now therefore go to, proclaim in the ears of the people, saying, whosoever is fearful and afraid, let him return and depart early from mount Gilead. And there returned of the people twenty and two thousand, and there remained ten thousand.

And the Lord said unto Gideon, the people are yet too many; bring them down unto the water, and I will try them for thee there: and it shall be, that of whom I say unto thee, this shall go with thee, the same shall go with thee; and of whomsoever I say unto thee, this shall not go with thee, the same shall not go.

So he brought down the people unto the water: and the Lord said unto Gideon, every one that lappeth of the water with his tongue, as a dog lappeth, him shall thou set by himself; likewise everyone that boweth down upon his knee drink.

And the number of them that lapped, putting their hand to their mouth, were three hundred men: but all the rest of the people bowed down upon their knees to drink water.

And the Lord said unto Gideon, by the three hundred men that lapped will I save you, and deliver the Midianites into thine hand: and let all the other people go every man unto his place.

So, one of the first things we notice in this text is that those who were filled with fear were eliminated. Secondly, he eliminated those who were not utilizing wisdom and those who were not sold out for the cause. Those who were only focused on fulfilling their immediate physical needs were not in position to be used by the Lord.

In verse seven, the Lord speaks expressly, stating that by three hundred that lapped will He save you. In previous verses, he stated that this process was necessary that he may get the glory and that they wouldn't be led to feel as though they received the victory by their own strength. Those three hundred chosen were those who had no fear. They had no concern for their own lives. However, they were consumed with the same visions and were of one accord. When you have a mind-set to want to serve the Lord and you're consistently focused on doing things God's way and carrying out his will and purpose, you'll find yourself having more power than you could have ever imagined...power to accomplish anything! If God be for us, who can be against us?

Contrary to popular belief, the power is not in numbers...at least not in a way many think. The logical perspective shared by the world would have you entertain the notion that the more people you have in any particular instance, then the more of an advantage you have to penetrating an enemy's line of defense. However, Jesus Christ is not logical. He is faithful. Faith is what moves the Lord Jesus on our behalf as well as obedience. Jesus Christ requires a heart of surrender to his will in obedience. Though most people come desiring "the more", hoping for something so profound, the reality is in the simplicity of obedience to love him with our whole heart…the obedience to praise him…the obedience to trust him and lean not to your understanding.

When King David numbered the people and kindled the wrath of God, the sin wasn't numbering the people. The Lord God was provoked to anger because of our actions of unbelief as a nation. His hand is not shortened that he cannot save. However, faith moves him. Trust in the Lord with all of your heart. He is our refuge, a very present help in the time of trouble. Remember, we walk by faith and not by sight. We cannot depend on what we see with our natural eyes.

II Kings 6:10-18

And the king of Israel sent to the place which the man of God told him and warned him of, and save himself there, not once nor twice. Therefore, the heart of the king of Syria was sore trouble for this thing; and he called his servants, and said unto them, will ye not shew me which of us is for the king of Israel?

And one of his servants said, none, my Lord, O king: but Elisha, the prophet that is in Israel, telleth the king of Israel words that thou speakest in thy bedchamber.

And he said, God and spy where he is, that I may send and fetch him. and it was told him, saying, behold, he is in Dothan.

Therefore, sent the hither horses, and chariots, and a great host: and they came by night, and compassed the city about.

And when the servant of the man of God was risen early, and gone forth, behold, an host compassed the city both with horses and chariots. And his servant said unto him, Alas, my master! How shall we do?

And he answered, Fear Not: for they that be with us are more than they that be with them.

And Elisha prayed, and said, Lord, I pray thee, open his eyes, that he may see. And the Lord opened the eyes of the young man; and he saw: and behold the mountain was full of horses and chariots of fire round about Elisha.

And when they came down to him, Elisha prayed unto the Lord, and said, smite this people, I pray thee, with blindness, and he smote them with blindness according to the word of Elisha.

The enemies of the children of Israel became bewildered when the children of Israel had been warned of their whereabouts on numerous occasions. When you make it a priority to do the Lord's will and walk in his statutes, he reveals himself as a good shepherd toward his flock as our shield and buckler. He is our exceedingly great reward. All things work together for the good of those who are called according to his purpose (Rom 8:28). So, there is no need to fear what man can do.

Psalms 27:2-3

When the wicked, even mine enemies and my foes, came upon me to eat up my flesh, they stumbled and fell. Though an host should encamp against me, my heart shall not fear: though war should rise against me, in this will I be confident.

No matter what enemy attempt to set a snare or trap for us, Jesus will lift up a standard. The Lord has his servants with intel for our protection. There is not type of weapon or strategic plan of action that the Lord will allow to prosper. In the mentioned passage with Elisha, though the enemy sent a host to compass the city by night; Elisha prayed to the Lord. The prayer was special because it wasn't regarding the way the Lord would handle the enemy. He wanted to strengthen the confidence of the servant of God. He needed a little more faith to endure through that trial. The Lord had already gifted Elisha with the ability to discern what the servant of God needed. He needed to see with his spiritual eyes that he wasn't alone on the battlefield. He needed to see that Jesus had him covered. Because of Elisha's obedience in faith to pray, the Lord answered and revealed to the young man of God the spiritual battlefield full with soldiers of the Most High, ready, and willing to fight on our behalf. So, let faith abound. Don't give up in the midst of the Lord trying to build you on your most holy faith.

Few Chosen

The Word states that many are called but few are chosen. When the Lord calls, be sure you answer. If you don't answer and "step up to the plate", then how can he choose you? We learned from the account of Gideon mentioned earlier that you must have a submissive and faithful heart for the task.

Though the Lord's body has many members which cannot be numbered, most missions or "task forces" are often organized in smaller numbers. Special forces are often considered positions of higher skilled level servants. Though they have special training and gifting spiritually, they have attained to a greater portion of humility just as well. To whom much is given, much is required. We see an account of this with Jesus in Matthew 17:1.

Though Jesus had twelve disciples, Jesus took only three apart into a high mountain. Those three being Peter, James, and John. There, they get another revelation of Jesus Christ and were privileged to see the transfiguration there.

When the Lord is taking you through higher heights and deeper depths, there is a spiritual training and there aren't many with the same spiritual hunger to go through the refining fire with you. Even if you want them to go. They cannot. Trust your chief. He is your creator. He is the first, the last, the beginning and the end. He knows the plans that he has for you. They are to prosper you and to bring you to your expected end.

BEHIND THE ENEMY LINES

As we have learned, there are at least two sides in warfare. For a brief moment think about the game of chess. In chess, there are levels to the line of defense. On the first level, there are pawns. The second level is where all of the high-ranking officials reside. There is the knight, rook, bishop, queen, and the king, all of which have a great deal of power and authority. The entire objective is to penetrate the opponent's (enemy) line of defense and render the king powerless and unable to function with nowhere to go (mate). Our spiritual warfare is somewhat similar. As we continue to grow spiritually the Lord continues to add to the amount of power and anointing he entrusts us. With this power comes a great deal of responsibility. See, usually in warfare the little people aren't the main target. Those who don't have much anointing power are simply used to gain access to the most secured lines of defense. Once the high-level security is breached, then an opening is left and a potential threat to take down the armor bearer and those in the inner circle of the main target. If your enemy can penetrate your inner circle and armor bearers, then this grants access to annihilate you!

Some of the ways in which the enemy will try to penetrate your lines of defense is by first trying to get what you love and by bringing your past front and center. Most of us can agree that when issues begin to arise with regard to what we love—whether it's family, friends, or even a career—we can easily get sidetracked into reacting emotionally and irrationally. This is what the enemy wants us to do. However, we must understand beyond feeling and emotion that everything has a spiritual design. We must stay focused and recognize the different spirits in operation. I know this seems easier said than done, but this is warfare! This is not for the faint at heart.

I had a situation where I was faced with the loss of my children in a custody battle from my first marriage, which was not ordained by God. I had to make a choice. Was I going to take up my cross and walk in faith? Or was I going to give up all hope, grow bitter, and allow hate to surface in my heart and lead to my utter destruction? Would I walk in the Spirit or would I walk in the flesh? My enemies as well as the Lord knew how much I loved my children, but the ultimate question was how much did I love God? I chose God, and I had to stick with it without wavering and without compromise. The enemy will always hit "below the belt." It will never be merely a small thing. He knows what you love and will use a "by any means necessary" approach to take you out. Soon after I made the decision that no matter what the enemy did, I was going to be obedient and faithful to the Lord Jesus, the enemy pulled from the bottom of the deck with my past. With me a lot of what I love, and my past are tied together, which can make for double the trouble. Nonetheless, the main spirit the enemy sent to try and stymie my growth was the spirit of guilt; guilt brought his buddies shame and fear.

In the beginning of my first marriage the relationship started on a lie. I led the gentleman to believe that I was older than I was, and he resented me for that. I was young, and I didn't think about how my foolish decisions could affect someone else's life. I was selfish and found that certain things which seemed not to be a big deal to me were a very big deal to him.

After the relationship eventually came to an end, guilt played a major factor. Everything fell apart, I was on the brink of losing my children, and the enemy was having a party. Oftentimes, the enemy would place thoughts in my mind like "That's what you get," and "If you never would've lied in the beginning, you wouldn't be in this mess." I felt horrible for all I ever did wrong in the relationship even after repenting, and the enemy with his demonic forces continued to throw their fiery darts for as long as they were effective. The entire situation was embarrassing, and I feared the rejection of family and friends as I watched my life as I knew it unfold before me. There was nowhere to run and nowhere to hide.

Warfare is long, dirty, and you must enter in prepared to endure to the very end. With you being the target, spouses, close family, as well as friends (including church members) in your inner circle are subject to being used by the enemy to get to you. You must be armed and guarded at all times. Never put your weapons down…for anyone. Not everyone can go with you. Again, I will say that only the strong will survive and will stand. The weak must be strong. I don't care how much you love them; they cannot go! The weak will get you killed or give up your position. If you truly love them, then rid yourself of them to avoid fatalities, otherwise everyone will die!

Simon Peter said unto him, Lord, whither goest thou? Jesus answered unto him, whither I go, thou canst not follow me now; but thou shall follow me afterwards.   John 13:36

Our government and other governments use torture tactics and techniques for captured enemies in order to get desired intelligence and other pertinent information about our enemies and their allies. The process is exhausting and painful, which is an absolute understatement. There's blood, sweat, and tears. In the end, either they get the information they need, and the POW (prisoner of war) is killed, or they don't get the information and the POW is often still killed. However, none of this takes place without the POW being threatened with the fact that their loved ones will be captured and tortured as well if they don't break. This is why you must be sold out for the cause and fear not what the enemy will do. You must be willing to die to fulfill the mission.

Some of the things that come up when a POW is being tortured are "Where did you come from?" or "Who is your target?" The torture will continue until the questions are answered. The information given, if any, will definitely be verified. Even though in spiritual warfare our main enemy is Satan, oftentimes we need to keep in mind that he will send his demons and evil spirits to launch attacks on us. In some cases, they are sent directly from Satan, and in other cases they may be sent by someone working witchcraft, sorcery, or a worker of iniquity (explained in detail later on). Once we learn of the origination of a plan of attack, this is when we are able to "kill on contact" certain issues as discussed in previous chapters. The operations of the enemy must be nipped in the bud and brought to halt immediately. Do not pass go, do not collect $200, go straight to hell from whence you came! Nonetheless, the key is not to get caught behind enemy lines. Be sure you continue living in holiness and righteousness as you are called to do. We must also be found in the place we're supposed to be and doing what we're supposed to be doing. Stay heavily armed at all times, and I say again…never put down your weapons. Please understand that warfare behind enemy lines is great!! Meaning, dangerous and high-risk.

I have seen the wicked in great power, and spreading himself like green bay tree. *Psalm 37:35*

The power on the other side is unimaginable. Oftentimes, we can miss how powerful it really is if we don't stay spiritually sensitive. However, we must still know that greater is He that is in us, than he that is in the world (John 4:4). We must know who we are and know the power we possess. Everyone is not called or equipped to go behind enemy lines. This is why the Lord reminds us in His Word that we are many members of one body (I Corinthians 12:12). It is one thing to stand prepared and ready should the enemy come into your territory; it is a whole other ball game when you decide to cross into the territory of the enemy. As I mentioned earlier, we need to be sure we are in the right place at the right time. This means that we can't try to operate in positions that we are not called to operate in or trained to operate in. Operate in your own calling and be ever ready in season and out to utilize your weapons and fight in your appointed time and season. All warfare is not the same. Of course, we have our daily warfare. However, some situations warrant for a special operations unit to intervene. This type of operation going behind enemy lines by specially trained warriors who are on high spiritual levels and are anointed for such a purpose.

In a natural sense, you may recognize our US Navy SEALs, who operate in similar positions and have the same duties and responsibilities as our spiritual special ops warriors. Our Navy SEALs are considered a special warfare operation. They conduct secret missions that require them to go behind enemy lines. They capture enemy targets and intelligence and are also equipped for unconventional warfare. Our seals may also spy out territories of potential threats that have not been officially confirmed as enemies. Spiritually God has called many for such a task. However, few are chosen. Those who are assigned to these operations are highly trained. These soldiers have been through some things and have the endurance required to complete the missions. They have extremely close relationships with the Lord and have full-blown faith without doubt or wavering. These soldiers know what the commander would have them do, even placed in situations where the lines of communication are broken, and they need to operate without instruction. For these reasons, not everyone can go behind enemy lines. However, we can pick up our weapons and fight. We must stay heavily armed and dangerous. Fear not what man can do. Keep our minds on the things above so that we are constantly renewing our strength, abounding in love, and not growing weary in our well doing.

On certain occasions there is a necessity to go behind the enemy lines. A highly trained soldier will travel into enemy territory for such reasons as to deliver a message, to spy the land, to rescue someone, to take someone captive, or to eliminate them with a surprise attack. Any mission behind enemy lines carries a high risk of fatality and should be considered dangerous. We all have a mission to uphold. Every day we strive to fulfill that mission, whether spiritual or natural.

While attempting to abide in the will and purpose of Christ and be effective gatekeepers, there are appointed times when we have to go behind enemy lines for the purposes of delivering a message. The Lord Jesus Christ has sent his holy prophets to deliver messages of warning on behalf of his chosen people on several occasions. The Lord Jehovah is our refuge and our shield. He sent Moses to warn Pharaoh to let his people go. These actions were done so the Lord God would show himself as a deliverer to his children. The Lord's servants went into enemy territory in obedience to orders from the Most High. Do not go into the enemy's camp without good reason and a plan of action. Another reason for going behind enemy lines is to spy the land. The Lord sent spies into the land that he promised to the children of Israel before they were to go in a occupy and build. Though the Lord had given a promise, the promise was worth fighting for. The people in the land had to be moved out of the way. The Lord God gave instructions and warfare was necessary to obtain the promise. The Lord told Joshua in an instance to fear not and be of good courage because he was with them. The spies were sent to give confirmation of the Word of the Lord God and so that they could plan to infiltrate the land and seize it.

    We are many members of one body. We must operate in our purpose to stay covered. Do not leave your hedge of protection to do a job you are not ordained to do. Make sure you're backed by the Spirit of God. If God be for us, who can be against us? While in warfare, a soldier would take the risk to go behind enemy lines to rescue someone. Jesus Christ set the standard for this type of operation when he descended into the lowest parts of the earth and he preached to the saints who had died and he also took the keys of death and the grave from the adversary. Because of that act of love, death has no sting, and the grave has no victory. He has the power to lay down his life and the power to pick it up again.

    In certain situations where there are people who need to be rescued, go in equipped and prepared for such a task. A rescue mission requires a certain level of skill and training. You must be prepared offensively and defensively. You need the Holy Spirit to lead and guide you through situations like these. POW's are in extremely vulnerable positions and if you as the rescuer are not careful, they could become a casualty of war. The warfare we fight is a spiritual one. These battles are not natural! These souls are to be handled with care; they belong to Jesus Christ. Rescuing someone doesn't have to be done in a sense. Jesus Christ can use you to rescue someone with praise and worship. Paul and Silas were set free with praises to Jesus. Sometimes the Lord will use you to rescue someone through prayer for them. The effectual fervent prayers of the righteous availeth much. Love covers a multitude of sins. With utilization of our spiritual gifts and our spiritual weapons we can show up behind enemy lines in the spiritual realm and naturally not going anywhere. However, the warfare is real, and the danger still exists. You must be led by the Spirit to avoid any unnecessary warfare on your life.

    Taking someone captive is another reason for going behind enemy lines. It is a strategic warfare tactic of the opponent to take a hostage or "prisoner of war" in order to get the adversary to surrender or compromise. On occasion the "POW" made be used to get intel so that the captors can gain an advantage over their enemy. There are several biblical accounts where the prophets and disciples of Jesus Christ were delivered up to the high priests and counsels because they were speaking the Word of God and working the works of Christ. They were interrogated, beaten, and persecuted for his name sake. Besides wanting to capture someone, the only other reasoning for showing up on their turf is to take them by surprise and eliminate them while they least expect it. Follow the instructions of the Lord Jesus.

CAMOUFLAGE

A form by which a person uses to blend into their surroundings is known as camouflage, camouflage was worn as a uniform upon the outward appearance during times of warfare to avoid being seen by the adversaries spying the land or approaching behind enemy lines.

For there are certain men crept in unawares, who were before of old ordained to this condemnations, ungodly men, turning the grace of our God into lasciviousness, and denying the only Lord God, and our Lord Jesus Christ.

Jude 1:4

If our enemies cannot penetrate our lines of defense from the outside, then they will attempt to bring your operation down from the inside out. The Lord warned us of the wolves in sheep's clothing. Many carry with them the Christian title, but aren't a bit more saved than the demons in hell. Their names aren't written in the book of life, they are not called by God, and they never will be.

In the military were given a few different types of uniforms. In particular, our everyday uniform, we called fatigues. Of course, the uniform has since evolved, but I remember our main everyday uniform having several shades of green. These colors were designed to somewhat blend with our outer surrounding. For deployments to desert locations there was a different uniform which imitated desert-like environments. These uniforms gave us the ability to camouflage our existence and somewhat mask our appearance. In spiritual warfare we will have the same issues with people regarding camouflage.

The enemy has three agendas: steal, kill, and destroy. Once he is rendered unsuccessful from his outward approach, he will send spies and assassins to infiltrate from within. Keep in mind that our enemy has been around for thousands of years. He knows us better than we know ourselves. He has observed what we like and what we dislike and will attempt to use such knowledge to his advantage. Though enemies will attempt to mock and imitate what we do, we remain tried and true. Many have attempted to spy out our liberties that we have in Jesus Christ. Regardless of the situation or circumstance they aren't the only ones who are able to hide in plain sight!

What will it take to penetrate your inner ranks? How does a stranger get in and get you to drop your guard? Spies will learn your entire working and operation. They will walk like you, they will talk like you, they will pray like you. They will care about all the things you care about…all to get in…yes, I said pray like you. They will even speak in an unknow tongue, prophesy...whatever it takes. They will do what is necessary to blend. Time is not of the essence; there is no rush. The process for them is handled with patience and thoroughly calculated.

As a teenager, being my father's only child and the eldest of three children by my mother, there were times when I felt neglected. I rarely saw my father, and I wasn't very close with my mother. I was starved for attention and affection. I didn't feel loved. My heart was void, and I felt alone. No matter how much I was around friends and family I was lonely inside and felt rejected. The enemy watched from the outside year after year. He could see my pain. He could hear my cries at night when no one else was around. When times became really bad for me emotionally and there was no one to talk to, I began to write it all in a journal. I wrote down all my hurts, pains, feelings, and desires. The devil was right there reading every word of it. Once it's written, it's spoken! So, what the devil did was use all the information he had (my weaknesses were exposed), and he came up with a plan to get in and wreak havoc in my life.

I came in contact with a gentleman who was in the military. He was tall, built, and handsome. I loved his body, his personality, and when he was in uniform, he could do no wrong in my eyes. The enemy knew just what I needed, or I should say he knew what to present me with. This gentleman began to spend time with me, listen to my thoughts, ideas, and concerns. He told me he loved me. Temporarily my void seemed to be filled and the love I desired was given to me in an imitation form. I began drinking, fornicating, and Jesus became the last one on my list of priorities. I put my weapons down and slowly began on a downward spiral toward hell.

There is nothing like the real thing! Jesus is the real thing! The enemy will do all sorts of things to present himself as being an angel of light in order to permeate your most secured lines of defense and ultimately bring your most effective warfare to a halt. By willingly participating in sin, you are willingly committing mutiny against the Lord, who is considered your savior and commander in chief. This is open rebellion and refusal to obey orders. So, I had fallen and become useless in the army of the Lord.

Beloved, believe not every spirit, but try the spirits whether they are of God: because many false prophets are gone out into the world. 1John4:1

Understand that man cannot elevate you. Man cannot fill your voids, and when needs are being met, you must make sure that they are being met by God and that things are not being camouflaged or are an imitation of the real thing. If we are in constant communication with the Lord and continue seeking the face of God, being led of His Spirit, we cannot go wrong, and we will not be deceived. Try the spirits whether they are of God and know that all things will work together for the good. Self-evaluate and know your weaknesses. There comes a time when the weak must say they are strong. If you know your weaknesses, then most likely your enemy does too. Strengthen every crack in your foundation so that the enemy is incapable of entering it.

So built we the wall; and all the wall was joined together unto the half thereof: for the people had a mind to work. But it came to pass, that when Sanballat, and Tobiah, and the Arabians, and the Ammonites, and the Ashdodites, heard that the walls of Jerusalem were made up, and that the breaches began to be stopped, then they were very wroth, and conspired all of them to come and to fight against Jerusalem, and to hinder it.
Nehemiah 4:6-8

Therefore set I in the lower places behind the wall, and on the higher places, I even set the people after their families with their swords, their spears, and their bows. And I looked, and rose up, and said unto the nobles, and to the rulers, and to the rest of the people, Be not ye afraid of them: remember the Lord, which is great and terrible, and fight for your brethren, your sons, your daughters, your wives, and your houses. And it came to pass when our enemies heard that it was known unto us, and God had brought their counsel to nought, that we returned all of us to the wall, every one unto his work.

Nehemiah 4:13-15

We will be tried in our areas of weakness, so strengthen yourself. Let the strong bear the infirmities of the weak so that all can stay on the wall and fight the good fight of faith. Bear the burdens on one hand and hold your weapons in the other. The warfare is great, but God is even greater! Pick up your weapons…and fight!

Psalms 91

He that dwelleth in the secret place of the Most High shall abide under the shadow of the Almighty. I will say of the Lord, He is my refuge and my fortress: my God; in him I will I trust. Surely he shall deliver thee from the snare of the fowler, and from the noisome pestilence. He shall cover thee with his feathers, and under his wings shalt thou trust: his truth shall be thy shield and buckler. Thou shalt not be afraid for the terror by night; nor for the arrow that flieth by day; Nor for the pestilence that walketh in darknes; nor for the destruction that wasteth at noonday. A thousand shall fall at thy side, and ten thousand at thy right side; but it shall not come nigh thee. Only with thine eyes shalt thou behold and see the reward of the wicked. Because thou hast made the Lord, which is my refuge, even the Most High, thy habitation; there shall no evil befall thee, neither shall any plague come nigh thy dwelling. For he shall give his angels charge over thee, to keep thee in all thy ways. They shall bear thee up in their hands, lest thou dash thy foot against a stone. Thou shalt tread upon the lion and adder: the young lion and the dragon shalt thou trample under feet. Because he hath set him on high, because he hath know my name. he shall call upon me, and I will answer him: I will be with him in trouble; I will deliver him, and honour him. With long life will I satisfy him, and shew my salvation.

We are in a lifetime of spiritual warfare. However, we must keep at the surface the reason why we fight. This is about an everlasting relationship with our father and savior Jesus Christ. He is our peace in the midst of the storm. He is our refuge and our shield. He states that we can always go to him. He is our secret place where we can hide in the shadow of his wings.

Camouflage is also used to conceal a person's personality and true intentions. For these reasons it is so important to receive the gift of the Holy Spirit. The Holy Spirit searches the deep things, the very deep things of God. By His Spirit he gives us the ability to discern the spirits, whether they be righteous or not. We need his spirit to reveal spiritual camouflage of enemies with intent to harm.

Just as the enemy uses camouflage to hide in plain sight, Jesus gives his children the ability to hide in the midst of his Holy Spirit. He said for us to put on righteousness so that he sees himself and not our wretched flesh. His Spirit is a refuge where we can escape from the cares of this life. By hiding ourselves in Christ we are able to persuade men and women to come to Jesus for the remission of sins. We are able to be whomever we need to be to build the kingdom of God and for the sake of doing the Lord's will and purpose.

1 Cor 9:19-22

For though I be free from all men, yet have I made myself servant unto all, that I might gain the more. And unto the Jews I became as a Jew, that I might gain the Jews; to them that are under the law, as under the law, that I might gain them that are under the law. To the weak became I weak, that I might gain the weak: I am made all things to all men, that I might by all means save some.

Though the Jews were a small nation chosen by God, many needed to receive the Gospel preached that Jesus had indeed come as the Messiah and had died and risen for their sins. It is not any easy task to approach someone and teach on something so personal as iniquity and transgressions. However, camouflage presented in a way where you condescend to the lowly estate and present yourself on common ground gives a higher probability of being received.

   Jesus meets us right where we stand. He knows what we need, and he knows how we process things. Even for those seemingly without the law, Jesus has shown us a standard in showing empathy and understanding when encountering folks who may have had a different walk of life than we have. Jesus, too, came in the form of a servant so that he could gain the more. For these reasons many of the pharisees could not comprehend and rejected Jesus because he approached the people in such a humble way. He has given us gifts and talents to be what we need to be to compel men and women to come to Christ. So, let's remember to put our flesh under subjection and let our light shine forth that men and women would see our good works and glorify our father in Heaven.

PROMOTION TO THE NEXT RANK

Whether you're enlisted in the military or you're an officer, there's still a desire for more. You want to move up the ranks and also to receive more pay. If you're enlisted, you want more stripes; if you're a general, you want more stars and so on. With each promotion there are more duties and responsibilities.

In the spiritual aspect, additional duties and responsibilities require more power as well as more training. Furthermore, power and training come through experience. There are no shortcuts. In the military ranking system looking from a general standpoint, there are two main categories: enlisted(non-commissioned) and officer. Of course, there is more to it, but for now we'll keep it general. The enlisted usually starts at E-1 and goes even as high as E-9. The officer ranking usually starts at 0-1 and continues likewise. In many cases when being enlisted in the military recruiters often want to have you start out at E-1 unless you have some prior training and knowledge in your field which would warrant entering with a higher ranking. They will take into consideration prior college credits and the sort. The need to fill positions in your field of employ may be a motivator as well. Spiritually, there are many similarities. Once you initially get saved then you are a new convert. After some gain of knowledge, teaching, and receive the Holy Spirit you become a saint, then from saint to lay person and so on depending on the will of God.

Previously, we spoke of boot camp and that process. Nevertheless, after making it through boot camp you're still released as your initial enlisted rank. To be promoted to the next rank you simply must do the work. I think many would agree that before a promotion you're usually already familiar with the ins and outs of the next position and are able, willing, and operating in that position before the title is given.

Along with this, let me also state that obedience is required! Most promotions when earned properly are given because the person up for promotion is seen working diligently in their line of duty to complete the tasks and responsibilities assigned as they pertain to the overall mission. They don't have to be told over and over to do things. These individuals are proficient (rarely making mistakes) and accountable when there are questions or concerns that may arise. The same goes also for spiritual promotion. We know that we need power, and that power is given through promotion. To get to the next spiritual level you must master the level that you're on, be seasoned for a while. With the power that you currently have, use it!

As trials, tribulations, and challenges come your way, fight the good fight of faith and utilize the weapons you've been given. You cannot avoid your duties and responsibilities and then expect to be given more authority and power. When faced with difficult situations, you can't run. The scripture reminds us that we will reap if we faint not (Galatians 6:9). We must press; failure is not an option. If the Lord tells you to do something, then do it. Get a full understanding of what the instructions are or what God is requiring of you and then follow through with actions without wavering and with compromise or rationalization. Throughout all of your endeavors seek the face of God and do not lean toward your own understanding. As God begins to see that you're capable of handling the power and authority he has given you along with the responsibilities that come with that power, it is then that you can be trusted with more. The Word states that if you be faithful over a few things then. He will make you ruler over many (Matthew 25:23).

Power and authority come with experience. As you continue to grow spiritually and move up the spiritual ranks, you become the main target. If the head of any operation can be destroyed, then the foundation can be shaken and brought down. The head is the visionary and the pillar on which everything leans and depends. If the pillar cracks, then every weight that it bears will come crashing down also. This is why it's God's design that we don't start at the top of the ranks. We grow from faith to faith, strengthening the foundation from the bottom to the top. This way, no matter how much weight is pressed upon the foundational pillar, it will always stand!

As I stated, obedience is crucial when you're expecting a promotion to the next spiritual level. God wants to know that those he's entrusted with his authority are going to follow directions the first time they are given without deviating or altering the original plan or set of instructions. Stick to the plan. Victory always comes when all squadrons, regiments, platoons, brigades, or any other groups are all on one accord and in unity. Where there is unity there is strength. Lasting strength is what conquers enemies and breaks through strongholds. In every situation you face, stay the course. Do what you've been trained to do. Do not allow outside influences to cause you to have shortcomings. At the end of the day we want to be counted worthy. We want God to say, "Well done, thy good and faithful servant, not "Depart from me, you worker of iniquity."

Servant To Friend

As a soldier and servant of the Most High there has been placed within our spirit man a desire for "the more." The Lord has given us the desire to seek for the end result of our works of righteousness. The word is given in Hebrews

11:6, but without faith it is impossible to please him; for he that cometh to God must believe that He is, and that He is a rewarder of them that diligently seek him. Having said that, there are several occasions in which the Lord Jesus Christ elevates his servants to the next level. These reasonings include faithfulness to seek him, obedience, and necessity.

It is such a joy to be elevated to the next rank whether spiritual or natural. What a feeling of accomplishment to have been acknowledged by the Lord Jesus Christ and by those in the natural having rule over us. However, though there is a reward for our endeavors and faithfulness to our mission, to whom much is given, much is required.

Though we acknowledge the word promotion or term elevation to mean moving up, some may consider from another perspective the aspect of decreasing. Spiritually, you are more of a servant. You take on more spiritual responsibilities that are considered your reasonable service. We love "the more." We endure hardness "the more." We pray "the more." We praise "the more." Keeping our affections on the things above, the Lord will reward us for our obedience to walk in his righteousness.

Col 3:22-24

Servants, obey in all things your masters according to the flesh; not with eye-service, as menpleasers; but in singleness of heart fearing God: and whatsoever ye do, do it heartily, as to the Lord, and not unto men; knowing that of the Lord ye shall receive the reward of inheritance: for ye serve the Lord Christ.

Even though we may have natural jobs or assignments, they are still ordained for a spiritual purpose. Therefore, the obedience and faithfulness is spiritual. The Lord is looking upon us observing the good as well as the evil. It is our reasonable service to do our works with the spirit of excellence knowing that the Lord our God is in the midst.

John 15:14-15

Ye are my friends, if ye do whatsoever I command you. Henceforth I call you not servants; for the servants knoweth not what his Lord doeth; but I have called you friends; for all things that I have heard of my father I have made known unto you.

The Lord elevates in the mentioned scripture from servant to friends. He declares that servants are not given to know what the master doeth, but the

Lord Jesus shares his will with his friends. Jesus considered us friends of his, we must abide in his love and keep his commandments.

There are numerous types of elevation in the spirit realm. The Lord does it according to his will and purpose and for his glory. Besides allowing us to go higher heights and deeper depths because of faithfulness and obedience, it is oftentimes a necessity for certain gifts and callings. For example, the disciples who followed Jesus Christ were given the promotion to Apostle. With that promotion they were Christian Pioneers given the authority to lay the foundation of Christ. With that elevation they worked signs, miracles, and wonders in his name to confirm the Word of God and establish the faith in those who would believe. Joseph also was elevated in the house of pharaoh so that he would be in the right position when the time of famine took place. When the Lord calls you, he qualifies you to do the job at hand. He will not put more on you than you can bear.

How Do You Receive A Spiritual Promotion?

When you're walking with Jesus, you're walking by faith in his spirit. You decrease so that his spirit may increase. So, in my opinion promotion oftentimes comes when you're not expecting it. You're just doing your job as a member of the body, humbling yourself daily at the foot of Christ.

Rom 1:11

For I long to see you, that I may impart unto you some spiritual gift, to the end ye may be established;

The Lord Jesus Christ uses his holy apostles and prophets to impart spiritual gifts so that we can continue to abound as effective members within the body of Christ. The impartation is accomplished with the laying on of hands. The prophet of the Most High may also at the appointed times speak the will of God into your spirit.

1 Tim 4:14

Neglect not the gift that is in thee by prophecy, with the laying on of hands of the presbytery.

The Lord Jesus Christ also promotes through your praise with your whole heart. The more you praise him, you break down fleshly barriers. Your praise sheds weights and spiritual heaviness so that the spirit man can elevate, and you can receive through the spirit what the Lord has you to receive. Sometimes the promotion comes with gifts such as prophesy, interpretation of tongues, or whatever else the Lord wants to distribute by his spirit. Having been privileged to receive a gift from God, let us not neglect him but stir up the gifts that have been imparted unto us so that we as a body may elevate in Jesus Christ unto a perfect man, fit for the bridegroom.

Eph 4:12

For the perfecting of the saints, for the work of the ministry, for the edifying of the body of Christ: till we all come in the unity of the faith, and of the knowledge of the son of God, unto a perfect man, unto the measure of the stature of the fullness of Christ:

    We must remember that the Lord has a purpose for all things. Promotion is not done just for individuals, but for the edification of the entire body. The Lord's pouring into you will be used for the purpose of building someone else in the faith until we all come into unity as Christ has desired. Therefore, we must continue to utilize every gift and we can stand as the everlasting kingdom God called us to be.

HONORING THE FALLEN

First let me make mention that fallen does not mean failure. Many believers who have fought the good fight of faith and whose life has come to an end are counting on us. Those who overcome are the ones who receive the inheritance in the end. Nonetheless, those saints whose life has come to an end on earth are crying out, "How long must we wait, O Lord? How long, O Lord, will it be until the dreadful day when your enemies will be made your footstool?" We must fight the good fight, if not for ourselves, for those who have fought and sacrificed their lives for the mission.

In the natural, we honor our fallen all the time. We preserve special days such as Veterans Day, Independence Day, and even Memorial Day. On these days, we take the time out to remember those who were killed or wounded in combat and also those active duty and veterans who have fought and continue to fight to maintain our freedom as a nation.

In the spirit we must do the same. Many saints have been called home to Jesus. They have fought the good fight; they have finished their course. Nevertheless, they still have the expectation that the work must go on. We must carry on where they left off and preserve the military of Christ. How do we do this? We honor the fallen spiritually by not putting our weapons down. We must also be sure we are fighting on the correct side. Some people think they are on the battlefield for Christ, but they really are not. They have lost their way. Their fighting is in vain because they have begun fighting for the enemy, unawares. Remember the Pharisees, Sadducees, and the Scribes? Well, they knew the law inside and out, backward and forward. However, when Jesus came with healing, deliverance, and casting out devils they called him a blasphemer. They thought that by delivering him up to be crucified that they were doing God a service. They were caught up in rituals and traditions but lacked relationship. So, when Christ did come, they missed the boat. They didn't realize they were fighting on the wrong side. The Word didn't come alive in their hearts. Stay the course, saints, and don't put down your weapons.

Earlier I stated not to confuse fallen with failure. Many wars have been fought. Soldiers were wounded and died for the cause. However, we know that in Christ to die is gain when in the line of duty. Nevertheless, the mission was accomplished. Fight the good fight of faith.

Honor the fallen also by replenishing the Lord's Army appropriately. When soldiers return home to the Lord, they must be replaced. The war must go on until the Lord's return. In order to remain effective and not become outnumbered, we need to give unto the Lord his Godly seeds. This means that we can't be selfish and say, "God, I'm not having any children." Ask God what His will is. Also, for those of us that do have children, whether planned or unplanned, raise your children in the way in which they should go. Don't be lazy and allow them to be overtaken with the spirit of the age. Teach them the ways in which they should go, and they shall not depart from them (Proverbs 22:6), but they will grow to become mighty warriors for the Most High God. This task is not easy, but when the Lord is involved every step of the way, all things will work together for the good. They took prayer out of some of the schools, but not out of the home. Prayer is an effective weapon. Get everyone involved. Spew the enemy with your prayers as a family. Where there is a united front, there is strength, and it will push the enemy to retreat.

    Don't let your good be evil spoken of. Make sure you're being led by the Spirit and that your fruits are showing throughout all of your endeavors. Righteousness and Holiness are weapons of warfare also. Let your light shine, because through your righteous walk many will be saved. One of our missions is to win souls. Oftentimes, this happens just by people watching. Stay the course. Do things in decency and in order. The enemy is standing by waiting for you to mess up and deter someone from surrendering their heart because of something they have seen or heard you do wrong. The more holy you are, and the more you walk in righteousness, the more effective you are for Christ. There is nothing worse than someone praying for you and you finding that they can't even get a prayer through. Why can't they get a prayer through? They walk in unrighteousness. With Holiness there is power. You can't heal the sick without it. You can't raise the dead without it. You can't set anyone free without it (all in Jesus' name, of course!).

    Let's honor our fallen the right way. Carry the banner of Christ with pride. Let us run all, that we may obtain that promise which is the victory. Don't give up. The enemy would love for us to run out of strength and die in vain, even commit spiritual suicide. How do you commit spiritual suicide? By failing to truly believe, fainting, giving up, or turning back to old things even as Lot's wife did in the Old Testament. However, the Word asks us the question in Ezekiel 37, "Can these dry bones live again?" With a full heart of surrender, they can. Say yes to the breath of life from Christ and go on into perfection. When you feel strength beginning to dwindle, recite Philippians 4:8:

Finally, brethren, whatsoever things are true, whatsoever things are honest, whatsoever things are just, whatsoever things are pure, whatsoever things are lovely, whatsoever things are of good report; if there be any virtue, and if there be any praise, think on these things.

Fret not thyself because of evildoers, neither be envious of workers of iniquity. Do not put your weapons down. For Jesus we live and for Jesus we die. We've been given too many weapons to fail. Pick up your weapons...and fight! The victory is ours!

There are many saints who have preceded us of whom the Lord used to pave the way for us to walk in the righteousness of Jesus Christ. Several soldiers have been martyred while attempting to bring forth the wonderful plan of salvation. While it may seem as if their role as a member was simple, they had to overcome all manners of evil and adversity. The reward is in the finish. We must overcome and endure to the end. We shall reap if we faint not. We honor the Lord Jesus as well as our predecessors by finishing the work that the Lord used them to start. Remember, however, we are not honoring the flesh. We are honoring the Spirit of Excellence, the Holy Spirit, that they yielded to so that a spiritual work could be manifested in the earth.

John 5:36

But I have a greater witness than that of John: for the works which the Father hath given me to finish, the same works that I do, bear witness of me, that the Father hath sent me.

The works that the Lord Jesus Christ established here on Earth didn't end with his death on the cross and his resurrection. That was a standard of righteousness set forth as a testimony of Jesus Christ. His kingdom is an everlasting kingdom. Therefore, so is the testimony of his works. In our obedience to do his will, those works will continue to bear witness.

Are You Not My Work?

1 Cor 9:1-2

Am I not an Apostle? Am I not free? Have I not seen Jesus Christ our Lord? Are not ye my work in the Lord? If I be not an Apostle unto others, yet doubtless I am to you: for the seal of mine Apostleship are ye in the Lord.

When I started to walk in my Pastoral calling, I was full of zeal. Yet, I was very naïve. I did not have any desire for ministry or for a leadership position. However, the Lord humbled me after surrendering to his will and purpose. He showed forth miracles, signs, and wonders to elevate my faith and confidence in His Holy Word. There were several people of the cloth that I encountered. There were other Pastors, Teachers, Missionaries, and Evangelists. The Lord used many of them as examples of what to do and what not to do. He showed me oftentimes where his presence was and where he was not. To mention how naïve I was, is an understatement. I knew nothing. I still don't. The Lord Jesus Christ gave his Spirit to lead my life so his will could be done. When I say I had zeal, that's what I mean. I loved Jesus Christ. He changed my life. He healed me. He delivered me. He purchased me. My response was full commitment to do his will and purpose. I say again, I knew nothing. I was a child. I still am his child. I come to him as a child. Because I know nothing. He does everything!! All I know is to surrender. My will is to do his will. He gives the increase. He is the mender of broken hearts. He sets captive free.

There were a few sincere beings that the Lord used to encourage me as I learned to "die" and abound in the love of Jesus Christ. Those sincere few, true believers, were the other members of the body. They instructed me to walk in the path of righteousness. They prayed for me. They wanted his will to be done more than their own will. These sincere folks didn't look at flesh and blood and the weaknesses thereof. These faithful soldiers, my comrades, saw the end result of us being men as trees planted by the rivers of water that bringeth forth the fruit in the appointed season. They believed that all things were possible through Christ who strengthens us. That type of unity and purity of heart is what glorifies God. That is the letter written upon our hearts. Therein is the honor unto God. Therein is the glory.

God is love. The purified love of God is eternal and everlasting. There is no way to contain him into one small chapter. However, it is essential to mention the love of Jesus Christ and that the power therein is the basics of the spiritual battles we're fighting.

What most people tend to do sometimes without necessarily realizing it; they attempt to label or categorize the love of Jesus Christ. The purified love of Jesus exists in three persons: The Father, The Son, and The Holy Ghost. He is. It's that simple. God is love. He is. It's not a religious thing. He is the truth. He is. Love stands on His own as the originator of all things. There is none greater, so He swears on himself. He is the Ancient of Days. He is the all-seeing, all-knowing, God who is everywhere.

When you're in the midst of warfare, love is there. No matter the circumstance, no matter the situation, he is there. When you need someone to talk to, love is there. Love cannot be personified. Though he exists through most people, love is a spirit. It is necessary to understand because we cannot put our confidence in man. He will have short comings. The purified love of Christ is coupled with his Holy Spirit. The expectations of such a great gift cannot be compounded to the standards of man's wisdom. When you need love to present himself in your life, He is there. There is rarely any confusion of who He is. Love recognizes himself in others, when he's pure and true.

A Testimony of Love

As a young teenager the Lord Jesus Christ placed in me a heart of worship. I would attend Sunday services, and though I was a very shy person, I wanted to worship the Lord with the confidence that the others had around me. My passion for his presence was personal. I longed for him to manifest his presence upon me. I hungered and thirst for his righteousness. However, the worship I kept secret. I was heavy laden in sin, and I didn't want anyone to see my wretchedness. So, when I prayed, I found a secret place where I could pray to the Lord. Most of what I did was in secret. It wasn't just because I wanted to hide my faults and shortcomings, but I also walked with the perspective that no one love me or cared about me one way or the other.

On the outside things seemed to be alright. However, on the inside was bottled up hurt, pain, loneliness, frustrations, and misunderstandings. I misunderstood my purpose in Christ. I misunderstood the role that Jesus Christ was intending to have in my life as King, Father, and Savior.

I cried unto the Lord in my secret place. I must admit, however, that my prayers were somewhat selfish. I was a tattletale. I would tell on everyone and how they treated me. Then I would transition into telling the Lord how to bless me and to make this person and that person love me. I was rather comfortable with sharing my will with him. However, I didn't stick around to listen for a response or to even attempt to understand what his will was for my life. I would repent only to repeat in the same lustful activities the following week. It had become a pattern of sin and feigned repentance. My heart willing to surrender, but the foundation of my faith wasn't complete. I lived off of the testimony of others. I did not have my own encounter with the Lord Jesus Christ, though my heart yearned in desperation for the pouring of his Holy Spirit.

One evening I cried unto the Lord God with my whole heart. In this particular occasion I was done with everything. I didn't hold onto anything. I laid aside every weight and sin, every care and concern. I gave the Lord Jesus every burden and my whole life. I was convinced that the way I was doing things was wrong. I was not in control of my own destiny, Jesus was. As I cried to the Lord, I asked, "What is wrong with me?" and again I asked, "What is wrong with me?" then the Lord began to respond and share his will for my life when I completely surrendered my will to his. He said the most comforting words to me "There is nothing wrong with you" and then went on to share I needed his Holy Spirit to lead and guide me in the path of all truth and righteousness. He stated that the world system operated on covetous practices which is to say that they do not pray for things according to the spirit, but to obtain things according to the flesh. Then he poured his Holy Spirit upon me so that I could pray in his Spirit and his Spirit would lead and guide my decision making!

When I received the Holy Spirit, my perspective changed concerning my life in Jesus Christ. My desires changed as well. I hungered and thirsted for spiritual things. I desired to know more of the Lord, so I read the Word often. I prayed more often for others and for a spiritual understanding of things I had read. I began to compare spiritual things with spiritual. I wanted others to see him as I had seen him. I wanted them to have his Spirit as well. I had a great desire to see his miracles, signs, and wonders performed in the lives of others so they could have faith in him just as well. With his Spirit came zeal that I couldn't get rid of. I just wanted to do his will. I wanted revival in the community and everywhere I traveled. I knew that it wasn't me. The Spirit and I became one. I was moving by his Spirit and the flesh was under subjection. It was then I really understood that love covers a multitude of sins. (1 Pet 4:8)

And above all things have fervent charity among yourselves: for charity shall cover a multitude of sins.

    By his Spirit the Lord Jesus Christ cleansed me from the inside and out with his refining fire and made me new. He cleansed me of my faults and sins. He said he would remember them no more. He cast them into the sea of forgetfulness. All that Jesus had done in me, I carried as a testimony of the power of his grace and mercy. That love that was shown toward me; I knew if he did it for me, then he could do it for anyone else willing to surrender to his will and purpose.

    There was a designated time noted in the Word of God where his disciples began to ask him, "Who loves you the most?" and the response was, "The one whom I have forgiven the most!" I must carry the same purified love with me everywhere I go. Sometimes I sit and think on the goodness of the Lord and his tender mercies, and his loving kindness and I say to myself, "I am the one he has forgiven the most." Then, I ask "How can I love him more?" Though he has already given us the answer on numerous occasions. He stated that he has given freely and we, too, should do as we have seen our father do.

Luke 7:42-43 & 47

And when they had nothing to pay, he frankly forgave them both. Tell me therefore, which of them will love him most? Simon answered and said, I suppose that to whom he forgave the most. And he said unto him thou hast rightly judged. Wherefore I say unto thee, her sins, which are many, are forgiven; for she loved much: but to whom little is forgiven, the same loveth little.

    There is so much power in forgiveness and mercy. There's more than we can fathom in the natural sense. The power that comes in forgiving another does the heart like medicine. That kind of love works wonders in the spiritual realm. That kind of love had Jesus Christ die on the cross for our sins and rise again with all power in his hands with the keys of death and hell. That kind of love heaps coals on the enemy when you would rather show longsuffering and mercy rather than use carnal weapons.

John 15:10-13

If ye keep my commandment, ye shall abide in my love; even as I have kept my father's commandments, and abide in his love. These things which I have spoken unto you, that my joy might remain in you, and that your joy might be full. This is my commandment, that ye love one another, as I have loved you. Greater love hath no man than this, that a man lay down his life for his friends.

Jesus made it clear to us in his Word that we didn't choose him, but he chose us first. He loved us first. He loved us in a way that we couldn't comprehend. When he laid down his life for us, he called us friends. He loved us in advance. He saw the possibility of friendship and servitude in advance. He did all of this before we even knew him or knew how to love according to his Spirit.

Ephesians 3:13-19

Wherefore I desire that ye faint not at my tribulations for you, which is glory. For this cause I bow my knees unto the father of our Lord Jesus Christ, of whom the whole family in heaven and earth is named, that he would grant you, according to the riches of his glory, to be strengthened with might by his Spirit in the inner man; that Christ may dwell in your hearts by faith; that ye, being rooted and grounded in love, may be able to comprehend with all saints what is the breadth and, the length, and the depth, and the height; and to know the love of Christ, which passeth knowledge, that ye might be filled will all the fullness of God.

As I was reading the account of Moses on the mount one day, I dared to ask the Lord Jesus the very same question Moses did which was, "Lord, show me your glory." My prayer was that the Lord Jesus would glorify himself in me. However, I didn't realize that the answer to such a request could bring test and trials upon my life that I couldn't imagined. I suppose the quote "Be careful what you ask for…" didn't resonate in my mind until long after the request was made, and numerous times, I might add. The Lord says through the Apostle Paul that we shouldn't faint at the tribulations. These tribulations bring forth the glory of God in our lives. So, the Lord is sharing that the more we overcome the tribulations, the more glory is established in our lives. There is a requirement that we faint not. Then Paul prays on our behalf that we are strengthened by his Holy Spirit and might within our inner being. That by doing so faith is established in our hearts and we are rooted and grounded in the love of Jesus Christ. This is the recipe given to us that we may be able to know the love of Jesus and to somehow comprehend the breadth, length, depth, and height thereof. The Word is confirmed here through Paul that this kind of purified love passes all knowledge and therein we are filled with the fullness of God. That kind of love is the power of God unveiled. That purified love is the anchor of our faith. To see the Lord glorified in our lives much is required. In speaking scripture the Lord reminds us that to whom much is given, much is required. The zeal of the Spirit of God had me petition the Lord Jesus Christ on several occasions with request to "Take me up higher heights Lord Jesus." "Take me deeper depths in you O' Lord. I always commanded the more of his Spirit. There was much tribulation and continues to be troubles because of the passionate pursuit. The enemy doesn't want you to reach your destiny of righteousness in Christ Jesus. He doesn't want you to get your inheritance. The adversary cannot stand the glory of God. So as the faith and the glory are established through enduring these tribulations there is spiritual warfare to overcome.

Through every test and trial was the shedding of flesh. The higher heights and deeper depths required loss of self. The humility was established more and more. There was (and still is) great necessity to be completely saturated in his Holy Spirit. The Word says to live is Christ, to die is gain. I took up my cross and the self, had to die. With the loss of self, Jesus Christ reigns completely in unity with you by his spirit. Therein is the purified love of Christ. That kind of love is certainly worth fighting for.
1John 5:4-7

Whosoever believeth that Jesus is the Christ is born of God: and everyone that loveth him that begat loveth him also that is begotten of him. By this we know that we love the children of God, when we love God, and keep his commandments. For this is the love of God that we keep his commandments and his commandments are not grievous. For whatsoever is born of God overcometh the world: and this is the victory that overcometh the world, even our faith. Who is he that overcometh the world, but he that believeth that Jesus is the son of God? This is he that came by water and blood, even Jesus Christ; not by water only, but by water and blood. And it is the Spirit that beareth witness, because the Spirit is the truth. For there are three that bear record in heaven, The Father, The Word, and the Holy Ghost: and these three are one.

To experience the overcoming power of God and achieve the victory in battle you believe only and surrender completely to his will and purpose. Oftentimes, troubles come simply because we love. There is absolutely nothing that can separate us from the love of the Lord Jesus Christ. We must trust him completely. If we love the Lord, then we will obey his commands.

All of this love that the Lord Jesus Christ has poured upon our lives and the lives of the children of God was to lead and guide us to our expected end. The reward and the victory is in the finish. We must endure to the end.

The more that you seek the face of God and all of his righteousness, the more warfare the enemy will attempt to bring upon your life. However, God is the author and finisher of our faith. He is in control. He will not allow more than we can bear. The more we draw closer and know the Lord Jesus, the more the enemy will attempt to make us think we don't know him at all. That's where we walk by faith and know that we're in the Lord's hands. With the revelation of Jesus Christ there is much resistance from the enemy. However, we love the Lord more than our own life.

Revelation 12:11

And they overcame him by the blood of the lamb, and by the word of their testimony, and they loved not their lives unto death.

      Through Jesus Christ we have overcome the world. The victory in battle is given through the blood of the lamb and the word of our testimony, even unto death. We know these things because we are believers. Therein is the love of Christ and the power of God unveiled. That kind of love…that kind of victory is worth fighting for. So, PICK UP YOUR WEAPONS AND FIGHT!

AFTERTHOUGHT: THE CHASE

I thank God that He brought me to the next level in Him where I have a passion to seek after His face like never before. I am blessed with several spiritual gifts to be used for the uplifting of the kingdom of God. He is indeed a revealer of secrets and willing to show us the hidden things of Him if we seek Him for wisdom, knowledge, and understanding. I mentioned in the beginning how I wanted to serve my country and I had pride in my job; these things were transferred into pursuit for Him, all of Him in His glory, His favor, His righteousness…His way.

We're in spiritual warfare daily; that's why it's imperative that you utilize your spiritual weapons, spiritual armor, and spiritual authority. You can't leave home without them. Let me share something with you. I noticed that when I began a full-blown pursuit for the face of God, the Lord began to give me more and more spiritual insight to the deep things of God. The fight is really not a fight at all. The Lord shows you what is a battle and what is not worth fighting at all. Things of this world that once mattered don't seem to matter anymore. It reminds me of scripture, Exodus 33:16:

For wherein shall it be known here that I and thy people have found grace in thy sight? Is it not that thou goest with us? So shall we be separated, I and thy people, from all the people that are upon the face of the earth.

And the Lord said unto Moses, I will do this thing also that thou hast spoken: for thou hast found grace in my sight, and I know thee by name.

And he said, I beseech thee, show me thy glory.

And He said, I will make all my goodness pass before thee, and I will proclaim the name of the Lord before thee; and will be gracious to whom I will be gracious, and will shew mercy on whom I will shew mercy.

And He said thou canst not see my face for there shall no man see my face and live.

And the Lord said, Behold, there is a place by me, and thou shalt stand upon a rock:

And it shall come to pass, while my glory passeth by, that I will put thee in a cleft of the rock, and will cover thee with my hand while I pass by:

And I will take away mine hand, and thou shalt see by back parts: but my face shalt thou not be seen.

I desire to see the face of my commanding Officer, my Father, my Lord. I want to see Him in His glory as much as I can withstand. I'm seeking the Blesser, not the blessing; the Anointer, not the anointing; the Rewarder, not just the reward.

I believe that if I seek Him and His righteousness, all other things shall be added. I want so much of God that if I walk into a grocery store or into any public place, people will fall to their knees in repentance just because of the Spirit of the Lord upon me, so powerful that it breaks yokes, where people will cry out "What must I do to be saved?"

While I hardly consider the things concerning our seek an afterthought, Jesus Christ is the first thing…the main thing…the most important thing. You may have heard it mentioned that we don't have to "chase" the Lord Jesus. However, he has commanded that we seek him and live. We need to seek his spirit in order to be kept through these times. There are many books and supplemental materials that the Lord Jesus Christ has given to us teachers and instructors yet one father in Heaven. However, he is the only true source concerning the everlasting kingdom of righteousness. He is the first, the last, the beginning, and the end. He is the originator of all things. Those who truly have a passionate pursuit after God's own heart know that the hunger and thirst for His Spirit and his manifest presence cannot be quenched with mere knowledge of Him. The purified satisfaction only comes with complete unity in the faith by His Holy Spirit. You must have a personal relationship and be filled by His Holy Spirit.

Ephesians 4:12-13

For the perfecting of the saints, for the work of the ministry, for the edifying of the body of Christ: Till we all come in the unity of the faith, and of the knowledge of the Son of God, unto a perfect man, unto the measure of the stature of the fulness of Christ.

SUGGESTED SUPPLEMENTAL READINGS

THE POWER OF GOD UNVEILED
Pastor Tiara L. Hawthorne

GODCHASERS
Pastor Tommy Tenney

THE GOD CATCHERS
Pastor Tommy Tenney

PRAYERS OF A GOD CHASER
Pastor Tommy Tenney

Study Guide Question (Pre-Requisite)

There are situations that the Lord Jesus Christ allows to take place in our lives so that we come to a position of repentance.

1) What situation took place in your life that had you recognize Jesus Christ as your personal Lord and Savior?

_____

_____

_____

Sometimes there are things that we go through multiple times before we come to the knowledge of the truth and we lay aside the weights and sin that so easily beset us in the first place.

2) What obstacles did you overcome to allow the faith and grace of God to abound in your life?

_____

_____

_____

_____

3) When did you recognize a higher calling on your life and the need to be sanctified unto the Lord? What testimony was established in the process?

_____
_____
_____

I'M SAVED NOW WHAT?

Part 1 I'VE GOT TO GET MYSELF TOGETHER!

2 Cor 5:7 Therefore, if any man be in Christ, he is a new creature; and old things are passed away; Behold all things become new.

Matt 6:33 But seek ye first the kingdom of God, and His righteousness; and all these things shall be added unto you.

    A. SELF-EXAMINATION (REFINING PROCESS STARTS)
       1. Know the core of your personality
       Name three main personality traits about you that will absolutely not change.
       a)
       b)

       c)

       Name at least three things about yourself which need to change.
       a)

       b)

       c)

Some fleshly ex. of things which aren't Christ like: listening to secular music, smoking, drinking, shacking up, cursing, argumentative etc.
Some ex. of spiritual things which may need to change and be cleansed from the heart: lust, adultery, hate, unforgiveness, wrath, anger, depression, anxiety, and pain.

List some proposed ways in which changes can begin to take place.
       a)

       b)

       c)

Why do you do those things?
Examples: Stress, habit, want to forget about problems

a)

b)

c)

B. TACKLE THE PROBLEM HEAD ON!
(Now that we know what some of our issues are and what may be causing them, now we can face them one by one to avoid the enemy using these things against us) Before you can get your house in order, you must first get yourself together whether you're the head of the household or not.

Matt 7:3 *And why beholdest thou the mote that is in thy brothers eye but considerest not the beam that is in thine own eye?*

2 Chron 7:14 *If my people which are called by my name, shall humble themselves and pray, and seek my face, and turn from their wicked way; then will I hear from heaven, and will forgive their sin and heal their land.*

1. Humble yourself enough to understand that you are a child of the Most High and are called by His name.

2. Be Godly sorry. Meaning not just confessing with your mouth but believing in your heart! Turning completely not planning to ever do it again!

3. Pray and Seek the face of God, not just His hand, understand that He is seeking a relationship with you. You are His bride and He requires you to be without spot or wrinkle.

C. KNOW WHO YOU ARE IN CHRIST
"Seeking His Face Like Never Before!"

Isaiah 55:6 Seek ye the Lord while He may be found, call ye upon Him while He is near.

Jeremiah 29:12-13 Then shall ye call upon me and ye shall go and pray unto me and I will hearken unto you. And ye shall seek me, and find me, when ye shall search for me with all your heart.

1. Understand that before you were created in the womb God knew you and you were chosen and predestined to be who you are today.

2. Know that you are a peculiar people, separated by God, that you are not of this world, you're walking in foreign territory. However, you are here for a reason, everyone has a specific calling and works to do for the Lord.

Ezekiel 3:18-19 *When I say unto the wicked, thou shalt surely die; and thou givest him no warning, nor speakest to warn the wicked from his wicked way, to save his life; the same wicked man shall die in iniquity; but his blood I will require at thine hand. Yet if thou warn the wicked, and he turn not from his wickedness, nor from his wicked way, he shall die in his iniquity; but thou hast delivered thine own soul.*

2 Cor 4:3 *But if our gospel be hid, it is hid to them that are lost.*

John 21:15-16 *So when they had dined, Jesus saith to Simon Peter, Simon, son of Jonas, lovest thou me more than these? He saith unto him, Yea, Lord; thou knowest that I love thee. He saith unto him feed my lambs. He saith unto him again the second time, Simon, son of Jonas, lovest thou me? He saith unto him, Yea, Lord; thou knowest that I love thee. He saith unto him, feed my sheep.*

3. Make sure He is included in all of your plans. For the scripture states, that if we acknowledge Him in all our ways, He will direct our paths.

4. What gifts and talents have you been blessed with? Figure it out, seek God if you don't now and use them for the uplifting of the Kingdom. Even the small things are helpful like being able to decorate or sew or sing. Some people are exhorters, some are intercessors, some are servers, but all build the Kingdom. See 1 Cor 12:1. Know also that the Lord wants for His children to prosper and be in good health!

D. KNOW WHO THE ENEMY IS!

Ephesians 6:12 For we wrestle not against flesh and blood, but against principalities, against powers, against the ruler of the darkness of this world, against spiritual wickedness in high places.

1. The enemy comes but to steal, kill, and destroy.

2. He desires to have you, to sift you like wheat.

See Ezekiel 28:11-16
See Revelation 12:7-17

3. Utilize your spiritual weapons and authority God has given you.

2 Cor 10:4-5 For the weapons of our warfare are not carnal, but mighty through God to the pulling down of strongholds ;) Casting down imaginations, and every high thing that exalteth itself against the knowledge of God, and bringing into captivity every thought to the obedience of Christ;

Genesis 1:26 And God said, let us make man in our own image, after our likeness: and let them have dominion over the fish of the sea, and over the fowl of the air, and over the cattle, and over all the earth, and over every creeping thing that creepeth upon the earth.

Ephesians 6:14-19

a) Loins girded with truth

b) Breastplate of righteousness

c) Feet shod with the Gospel

d) Shield of faith

e) Helmet of Salvation

f) Sword of the Spirit

g) Praying in the Spirit

h) Garment of Praise

E. SOME RELATIONSHIPS MUST DIE

Genesis 12:1 Now the Lord had said unto Abram, get thee out of thy country, and from thy father's house, unto a land that I will show thee.

Unfortunately, everyone cannot go where the Lord wants to take you!

Exodus 33:16 For wherein shall it be known here that I and thy people have found grace in thy sight? Is it not in that thou goest with us? So shall we be separated, I and thy people, from all the people that are upon the face of the earth.

1 Pet 2:9 But ye are chosen generation, a royal priesthood, a holy nation, a peculiar people; that ye should shew for the praises of Him who hath called you out of darkness into the marvelous light:

See 1 John 1:5-7
Titus 1:16 They profess that they know God, but in works they deny Him, being abominable, and disobedient, and unto every good work reprobate.

Let your light so shine that others may seek your good works and glorify you father in Heaven. Let not your good be evil spoken of.

F. STAND FIRM ON YOUR FOUNDATION OF FAITH

1. Where is Your Faith? Believe Only!

Heb 11:1 Faith is the substance of things hoped for, the evidence of things not seen.

See Matthew 6:23-33

2. The shackles have been loosed.

See Mark 11:1-9

G. FINISH THE RACE

Our Lord has given us an overcoming Spirit.

Rev 2:7 He that hath an ear, let him hear what the Spirit saith unto the churches; To him that over cometh will I give to eat of the tree of life, which is in the midst of paradise of God.

See Rev 3:21

See John 19:30

NOTES

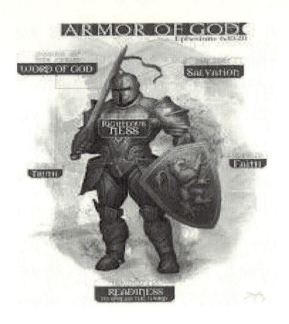

Made in the USA
Columbia, SC
19 March 2025